Mia's World

Mia's World

An extraordinary gift. An unforgettable journey.

Mia Dolan

with Rosalyn Chissick

Element
An Imprint of HarperCollins*Publishers*
77–85 Fulham Palace Road,
Hammersmith, London W6 8JB

The website address is:
www.thorsonselement.com

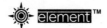

and *Element* are trademarks of
HarperCollins*Publishers* Ltd

First published by Element 2005

1 3 5 7 9 10 8 6 4 2

A catalogue record of this book
is available from the British Library

HB ISBN 0 00 718247 3
TPB ISBN 0 00 720408 6

Printed and bound in Great Britain by
Creative Print & Design (Wales), Ebbw Vale

Mia
*To all who are searching, may this book
help light your way*

Roz
For Mark, Hanna and Mackensie Michael Jones

Contents

Acknowledgements

Mia
I would like to thank:

Rosalyn Chissick for her courage and honesty.

All at ThorsonsElement, especially Katy Carrington, Liz Dawson and Belinda Budge, and everyone at L.A.W., with special thanks to Mark Lucas and Peta Nightingale.

And, of course – Eric.

Roz
Special thank you to Elisabeth Winkler for her tenacity with this project, her unerring instinct for the truth and all her help.

Thank you to Mercedes Nunez, Michael Chissick, Sally Adams, Lindsey Woloski, Alyson Hallett, Julie Mackinnon, Kathy Jones, Araminta Whitley, Peta Nightingale, Mark Lucas and Celia Hayley.

Prologue: Belief

Mia

I sat in a hotel room in Bath, waiting. In the year since the publication of my first book, I'd seen more hotel rooms than I had in the rest of my 42 years. I lit a cigarette, and glanced around the empty room. The curtains were heavy and shiny; the table set with cups and saucers. I thought of the warmth of my kitchen on the Isle of Sheppey, filled with the noise and liveliness of my family, my clients and friends. What was I doing here, miles from home?

People imagine psychics don't ask questions. We're meant to know everything but, although we are party to special and important information, we are still human. Stubbing out the cigarette, I got off the bed and padded around, hoping to relieve the wariness I could feel building. Catching sight of my reflection in the mirrored door of the wardrobe, I fumbled in my bag for my lipstick. The familiar ritual of applying it was calming.

I had been working as a psychic for more than 20 years, giving readings to a circle of people that grew by word of mouth as my practice developed. Now I was becoming a public face, a woman known for her psychic powers and, any minute now, a journalist from a leading magazine would arrive to interview me.

My daughter Tanya and I had read that magazine avidly, laughing at the gossip and glamour of celebrity lives. It was odd to think that now people wanted my story. But I had no illusions: our glories are transitory. Life is a wheel, bringing those at the bottom to the top – and, inevitably, down to the bottom again.

All the same, I felt apprehensive. I believe in what I do, and I didn't want my words misinterpreted by yet another close-minded journalist.

I jumped at the sound of the telephone.

'Rosalyn Chissick is on her way up,' the receptionist said.

A moment later I opened the door to a woman in her thirties, dark curls tumbling around an intense, yet friendly face.

Roz

Fifteen minutes before my appointment with Mia, I was sitting in the sun in a park, formulating questions for our interview.

'People seeing glimpses of the past or the future? Psychics are deluding themselves or the public or both,' I thought to myself. The vast psychic industry was probably an elaborate and lucrative scam. Nevertheless, I had to acknowledge another part of me – one that was open to being persuaded otherwise.

The idea of interviewing Mia had come from my editor. She told me that Mia had a remarkable reputation as a clairvoyant specializing in psychic predictions and hauntings. My brief was to try and discover whether her special powers were for real.

I did my homework. I found out that psychic readings attract all types: hard-headed business people, lost souls in search of guidance, curious dabblers wanting an intriguing party trick – even declared sceptics seeking logic-confounding truths. Psychic readings seem to imbue people with a sense of mystery, they feel party to a greater truth. We are fascinated by the unknown. It seems we all have a need to believe in something bigger – more powerful – than ourselves.

As I knocked on Mia's hotel-room door, I imagined a mysterious lady in a fringed shawl, but as the door swung open, Mia was no Gypsy Rose Lee. Tall with long blonde hair and a welcoming smile, her first words to me were 'Hello, darling.' She seemed open, and very down to earth.

Mia

I knew instantly that Roz was not impressed by anyone but respected everyone. And I knew that she was committed to the truth. There were no chairs in the room, but Roz quickly settled herself on the large bed, taking files out of her bag and rummaging for pens.

I busied myself, making tea with the hotel milk cartons and sugar sachets. Roz didn't mess around. Pen poised, she was ready to start.

Roz

'So, what was your first psychic experience?' I asked. Mia sat down and lit the first of many cigarettes.

Mia

I didn't know how Roz would respond, but she looked genuinely interested and this was a refreshing change from the rash of interviews that I'd done over the last few months.

'I was 22. I didn't believe in anything – God, ghosts, heaven, hell. I thought it was totally false – conjured up out of humanity's fear of its own mortality. Then one very ordinary day, I was trying to cook tea and the children were fighting in the front room, so I went in to see what was going on. Something caught my attention on the television. I was standing there watching it when, out of nowhere, a man's voice said, "Your toast is burning." I went into the kitchen and discovered that the grill pan was on fire.'

'I tried to put it down to reason – I told myself I had smelt smoke and must have imagined the voice. But over the next few weeks, the lights and my electrical appliances turned themselves on and off at will, the bed shook and the voice kept talking to me. I thought I was going mad.'

'I'd been brought up in an ordinary working-class family on the Isle of Sheppey. Things like this didn't happen to people like me. Eventually I went to see a doctor, who told me I was suffering from stress and gave me a prescription for pills. I was then sent to see a psychiatrist. The medical profession concluded that I was sane but strange and they left me to get on with it.'

'It took me eight months to find out that the voice (always the same voice) was my spirit guide, Eric. I know it sounds strange – and for years I told very few people about him – but Eric's presence shook my world; it changed me totally.'

'Before I met Eric, I didn't think about other people's problems. I didn't even consider whether something was a good or a bad thing to do. My dreams were to have a Mercedes and a house in the country. But becoming psychic made me realize that there was more to life and this had a snowball effect.'

'It helped me make sense of the things that had happened to me and gave me a purpose in life. I started thinking about yesterday, today and tomorrow. It made me pause; I stopped knee-jerk reactions to situations and started to think before I acted. Most importantly as I developed as a psychic, my priorities changed, I realized life has nothing to do with material possessions. The base line was: I stopped thinking about my life and myself and started to use that energy for other people.'

I told Roz how, over the years, I had come to know and trust that the voice belonged to a kind wise soul who had been sent to help me become a better person. The quality of her attention helped me touch on other parts of my life too. I was a protector, from an early age looking out for others. But I couldn't protect myself from pain or, ultimately, loss.

Roz
'Did your gift help you to cope?'

Mia
Roz was a strange mixture. Sometimes her questions were searching and tough. At other times she exuded such a strong sense of empathy that I wanted to tell her more about myself.

'At first, no. When my son died, I felt terribly let down. I shut Eric out of my life. I thought: "What's the point in having a psychic gift if it can't stop terrible things from happening?" Then something changed that. I gave a reading to a woman who had lost her daughter and I saw the comfort it gave her to know that her child's spirit was safe.'

'Nothing can take away the pain of bereavement, but knowing there is life beyond death, and knowing that she would see her daughter again, made the loss more bearable. This knowledge breathed life back into her love, and allowed her to bring the pain under control. In the beginning, being psychic was an adventure – now I see its true value to heal.'

There was a silence. Eventually Roz spoke.

Roz

'I still can't get my head around the idea that someone can see into the future. Can you give me proof that you have a psychic gift?'

Mia

There was only one way I knew.

'Shall I give you a reading?'

Eric doesn't always come when I do a reading but, as I began to tune into Roz, he was there straight away. His voice in my head was clear and strong.

'Eric says that you are on a spiritual journey yourself.'

* * *

Roz

I sat on the hotel bed opposite Mia, enveloped in her big presence and her warmth. I had interviewed many people in my career but the focus was always on the other person. They trusted me with their stories and I tried to honour that with my attention and receptivity. It was odd, then, to suddenly find myself under the spotlight.

I'm a private person – Mia's attention made me slightly uncomfortable. Yet in her first sentence she had connected me to a part of myself I didn't always have time to think about. I wondered if this was one of the reasons people went to see psychics: to focus on their lives and feelings, to spend a bit of time with their deepest dreams.

Since my late teens, I had been intrigued by the idea of a more spiritual life and interested in a holistic approach to health and well-being. Ten years previously, I had gone on a year-long round-the-world trip and been drawn to the spiritual traditions I found in India. There, life is lived on the street and everything is visible – the beauty and the brutality. People live very openly and their spirituality is relevant to the ups and downs of their everyday lives.

In India, for the first time, I met people who were devoting their lives to their spiritual practice. One very old man lived in a cave on a sacred river. He had nothing materially, yet every day he found a way to cook a meal for wandering beggars and *sadhus*.

In the Himalayas, I met Buddhist monks and nuns, exiled from Tibet. I took to heart their message that all the suffering and happiness in my life come not from external things like success or money but from my own mind – my own attitude. I met teachers who spoke of the need for loving-kindness towards ourselves and the importance of a fearlessly compassionate attitude to our own pain – and that of others. I soaked up teachings on honesty, kindness and bravery. Mia was right. I found the Tibetan Buddhist instructions gutsy and helpful – and, a decade later, I was still trying to put them into practice as well as I could.

Mia and I were off to a good start but, as we sat in silence, I wondered if people were impressed with the readings they received because they unconsciously, inadvertently coached the psychic. Desperate for reassurance, perhaps they ignored the irrelevancies and errors and, instead, exaggerated the insights and references that made sense to them. It might not even be manipulative on the psychic's part – but rather that natural human communication was given a supernatural spin by two parties desperate to believe. I understood the human need for certainty but if wool was being pulled over anyone's eyes, I wanted to understand that too. This reading was an opportunity to test Mia. I determined to give nothing away.

Mia

'I am going to close my eyes for a couple of minutes – nothing weird is happening, I am just relaxing. Then I'll open my eyes and we'll begin.'

'I'll start with a health scan. This will make you sound like you're ready for the knacker's yard but hopefully will only be light-hearted. I am going to start with your head. Your eyes are weeping and irritated … you have whiplash or muscular problems …'

Roz

There was no trance, no meditation, no holding on to objects that carried my 'vibrations'; Mia just looked into my eyes. But by the time she had finished scanning my health, my journalistic hat was firmly back on my head. Anyone who works at a computer will have tired, sore eyes, so no points for that one. And no whiplash or muscular problems I knew of, just the usual desk-bound, bad-posture backache.

Was it all going to be vague from now on? I felt the glimmerings of disappointment. Maybe my belief in a higher power was a childish desire to believe in magic. I settled back into my cynical comfort zone.

Mia

'I am going into the floater now. This will give me random images of things that have just happened or are just about to happen. The first things I see are wind chimes inside a door.'

Roz

I had brought a set of chimes back from Thailand – and for years now, they have been positioned inside my front door so that every time the door swings open, I can hear their sound.

Mia

'You are organized but chaotic. You're fiercely independent but, at the same time, you would give everything that you have away, given half a chance.'

Roz

It seemed that Mia was keying in, reading me. I began to see how people could give power to psychics. People often go for a reading when they have reached rock-bottom – they are distressed and their distress makes them vulnerable. Suddenly it can seem that a psychic has all the answers …

I made my face impassive.

Mia

'I see a fridge-freezer with a wonky door. I see you in Wellington boots looking at chickens. I see you putting on walking boots and you will be buying a new computer. And in the next two and a half to three years, you are going to be a well-known novelist.'

Roz

Mia was not looking at me. She had moved her head to the right as if someone else was talking to her. After a few moments, she laughed.

Mia

'Eric wants me to tell you that your characters have dreams and wishes as well as adversity. He says, "Let them win sometimes."'

Roz

Every once in a while, something comes along that, perhaps, you can't explain away. As a journalist, it was not a huge leap for Mia to assume that I had also written a novel, but how did she guess that my characters needed lightening up? My first two books had been called beautiful – but bleak. Only someone who knew my writing could have given me that advice. Had Mia read my book or did the information come from another source? The words were so pertinent, so right for me. I felt energized.

I looked around the hotel bedroom. The curtains – the table – looked sharper, clearer. If spirit guides really existed and could pass their wisdom to one human being to give to another, then perhaps there truly was a bigger picture.

Deep down, I knew I was not only testing Mia, but testing my own beliefs. I still wanted to know if the world I saw was the only one that existed or if there really was something more – something greater than us all. Suddenly there were a lot of possibilities.

Not everyone would be comfortable with the idea of sitting in a room with a woman who talked to a spirit from another dimension. But Mia made it seem so down to earth, so normal. The idea of Eric did not scare me. On the contrary, I was intrigued. I consulted my list of questions.

'Could you teach anyone to be psychic?'

Mia

'I could teach anyone to open up and be able to see. But I couldn't guarantee how far they could develop. Everyone has the ability to awaken their sixth sense, but there are varying degrees of ability. A child can paint a picture of a tree with a brown stick and a green blob. But a trained artist would paint with depths and hues that would make the tree come alive. You would get more clarity and information from the artist's picture. Similarly, some people would only be able to achieve a basic ability, while others could go on to full clairvoyance.'

Roz

As a journalist you have to follow your natural curiosity. And something about being with Mia was stirring me.

'Could you teach me to be psychic?'

Mia

'I just told you I could.'

Roz

'Well – will you teach me?'

It seemed to come out of the blue, but I was serious. I wanted to see how far we could take it – how far Mia was prepared to put herself on the line. I'd never witnessed any unusual psychic phenomena and didn't know if I believed in ghosts, but perhaps Mia could convince me.

I liked the idea of having a way to see into the future. Could I do it? But more than that, I wanted to know first hand – absolutely, no question – if there was more to life than what I could touch and see.

Mia

Would I teach her?

It is my belief – absolutely – that anyone can develop psychically, if you give them the tools. And if I could teach people to do it for themselves, then I could open them to receiving the understanding and comfort that clairvoyance gives me. It had always felt important that people could access that wisdom directly – with no middleman.

The truth was that for years I'd been nursing a dream of opening a psychic school. When I first became clairvoyant it was so scary and such a shock, that I feared I was losing my mind. So I wanted to create a place where people could go – a structured institution where they could learn that psychic ability was natural and they were not going mad.

Here I could teach people what it was all about and how to use the gift well; and then they could take classes to hone their new skills. I had spent hours imagining the curriculum: classes on how to receive information, others on how to interpret it. The most important thing would be that it was a non-denominational school – not attached to any religion, but somewhere that psychic skills were valued and taken seriously.

Developing psychic skills can benefit the world. The awareness that other people are feeling as strongly as you stops you living in the me-world. And from that, naturally, comes the desire to try to be of benefit. For that reason I have always wanted to bring psychic awareness to the forefront of society, to give it credibility.

In that moment, in an anonymous hotel room with Roz, I realized that I was being offered my first real opportunity along that path. She could be my first pupil, bringing the reality of the school that bit closer. I remembered my earlier trepidation about the interview. How differently things had turned out. My excitement grew. Looking at Roz's eyes and the way she interacted, her sensitive side was obvious. And, crucially, she was open-minded. I knew she would give it a proper go.

'The main reason people don't use their extra sense is because we have been brainwashed into believing it doesn't exist. Thousands of years ago, we would all have taken our sixth sense for granted, but we have now been programmed to ignore it.

Animals still use their sixth sense: birds know when to migrate, salmon swim thousands of miles home but humans have sadly lost touch with their instincts. Today, it is research, facts and statistical evidence that are most highly prized.'

'Young children often say they hear and see things, but most adults tell them they are being silly. This is the beginning of society pulling down the shutters. Teachers stop children from daydreaming, men tell women not to be 'illogical'. It is time we started valuing our intuition – it's our birthright and it's here to help us. All too often we ignore our hunches, yet if we could only learn to listen more carefully to our inner voice, we could drastically improve our lives.'

'Teaching you would take time and you would have to keep an open mind. If you learn with the thought that "it's not real anyway" then we will never be able to start. One of the major keys to unlocking the sixth sense is belief. The word belief appears in every major religious text. Belief is a magic word.'

Roz
Belief. Magic. Sixth sense messages. Why was I suddenly considering something so crazy? I was a journalist – I liked concrete facts. But, inside, two bits of me – the stern adult and the excited child – were battling it out. Despite myself, I felt thrilled, tingly. Who doesn't want to believe that magic exists?

'How long will it take?'

Mia
'Six months, from sceptic to psychic.'

Chapter I

—⚭—

Love and Loss

Mia

It took us a year to clear our diaries and find six months free for the training. I decided I didn't want to teach from my home on the Isle of Sheppey because there was too much going on. I live with my mum and my daughter, Tanya, which makes for lively chaos. There are always members of our extended family gossiping at the kitchen table. And then there are the friends and friends of friends, who turn up at the door asking for advice or readings. There is always something happening, so many people who need my time and care, and the door is open to them. I can't imagine living any other way, and I miss the bustle and the noise when I'm not there. But I needed a clear head and a place where I could devote myself totally to the business of teaching. I knew I needed to get away from home to find that peace and quiet.

I worked out that I could stay near where Roz lived, in the countryside outside Bath, for a few days every other week. Roz found me two places to choose from: a quiet hotel and an old English pub doing bed and breakfast. It didn't take me long to decide. I opted for the pub so I could watch TV and smoke in my room at the end of the day.

The drive from Sheppey took five long hours. Just outside Bath, I headed for the B&B. It seemed to be in the middle of nowhere. The building was over 100 years old, and the front was a riot of pansies in pots and baskets.

My room was basic and comfortable, with twin beds, a small bathroom and a dressing table. The window looked out over rolling hills and clumps of trees. It was very peaceful and I felt I'd be able to relax there.

I began the business of unpacking and settling myself in. I always make sure I have a light by my bed so that I can sit in its quiet glow and read before I go to sleep. The first thing I unpacked was my book. I can't go anywhere without one. I laid it on the bedside cabinet. Then I thought about where I was and it made me laugh: Pete and Shane would have loved this – me staying in a pub. But that could never happen now.

We lost my brother, Pete, when he was 25. He was stabbed in a pub when he was out celebrating his birthday with a group of friends. His loss devastated our family, and was a double blow to me because I had foreseen something happening and could do nothing to prevent it.

Some weeks before he died, Pete had asked me to give him a reading. I saw him with his fiancée, Angela, and his friends, out on a pub crawl. But then I saw a sudden scuffle, people moving very fast, and a flash of metal. I felt that Pete would be going away for a very long time, but when I told him – he just laughed. 'Ha. Did you hear that? Mia says if I go out for a drink, I'm going to end up in prison.'

Everyone loved Pete. He had a wicked sense of humour and although he'd been in and out of trouble, he was tough and loyal, and the best brother I could have asked for. When he met Angela, he fell head over heels in love. With the arrival of his beautiful daughter, Francesca, his world was complete.

The night he died, he was trying to protect a young friend from a group of seriously unpleasant men. When Pete stepped in to help, he was attacked with a machete. The post mortem revealed that the machete had gone into his liver, lung and spinal chord, but Pete still managed to take himself round the corner to the police station to get help. He collapsed at the desk and died from loss of blood in the ambulance on the way to hospital.

After I'd given Pete that reading, I felt a sense of dread. I tried to impress on him how serious it was – I wanted to stop him going out for a drink so that I could alter what I'd seen. It was so hard. I may be psychic, but I am human and vulnerable like everyone else.

Then, five years ago, my son Shane died. Eighteen years old, he was attacked while waiting for a train one night, and kicked in the head and chest. He survived the beating but, several weeks later, he collapsed. A scan revealed a massive blood clot and he had an operation to remove it. But it was all too late. He died, and no amount of begging and praying could bring him back.

When you lose a child you lose their future. I think about him all the time. I long to touch him, to hear him laugh, to see him loping about the house. I'll never forget how it felt to run my fingers through his hair, to trace the lines of his face, to hold him and smell him.

After Shane died, I was so angry that for a while I turned away from my gift. In my grief I couldn't understand the point of my sixth sense if I wasn't able to use it to help the people I loved. In my despair, I pushed Eric away and turned in on myself.

Then one day a woman came to me needing my help, and when I saw the sadness in her eyes, I knew that I had to try. And in spite of everything – all my pain and rage – the spirit of her daughter came to me very clearly. Afterwards, the woman hugged me and told me that I had no idea how much I had helped. But the truth was that she had no idea how much she had helped me. Through the deepest pain, I had learned the hardest lesson. Shane was safe, just as this woman's daughter was. Knowing there is life after death connects me to Shane. I know I will see him again, and that keeps my love alive. When I found it again, my faith was stronger than ever. I truly know that my gift is to help others.

Sitting on the bed in the pub bedroom, I began to see my path quite clearly. In publishing my first book, *The Gift*, I had told the story of my life and how I had learnt to live with and use my sixth sense. My gift was no longer private. Having travelled the country giving talks and appeared on television and radio, people now knew who I was.

Additionally, since the success of my book, I had been increasingly in demand. Each day brought fresh emails and letters, and many of them needed answering desperately. I was inundated with requests for readings from people who had identified with my story and sought comfort over the loss of their own sons, daughters, husbands, wives, brothers and sisters. There was such a need for psychic reassurance. It can be hard sometimes, but I have one important rule: when I'm working I give a hundred per-cent, and when I stop, my family get a hundred percent. And with each small piece of help I can offer, the path becomes clearer.

The past year had also been emotionally demanding. Dad died peacefully in his sleep and although Mum coped really well, she needed me. I was the family's problem-solver – the one everyone came to when they needed help, whether it was with filling in an insurance claim or healing a broken heart. There was always something to sort out.

Throughout the busy year, the thing that sustained me most was the thought of training Roz and, eventually, opening a psy-chic school. I trust in fate, and this felt like the next logical step in the process of bringing psychic awareness to a wider audience. I knew that the six months ahead were vitally important.

* * *

Finally, here I was driving to Roz's. Nevertheless, I had yet to work out a plan of action. In all the years I had been working as a psychic, I'd rarely thought about how I did it – the mechanics of clairvoyance. Teaching would mean developing a completely new set of skills. It was one thing daydreaming about a curriculum – quite another to break down what I knew instinctively into manageable steps for a novice.

When I thought of a 'teacher', I saw someone standing at the front of a classroom providing facts. But clairvoyance is not laid down in a set of rules. So much is based on experiential information. How was I going to communicate all this?

As always in situations like this, I turned to Eric for guidance. He is a constant – always there to help me learn, and to offer strength and reassurance.

'I think I need some help here, Eric,' I said aloud. (I only speak to him like this if I am sure I can't be overheard.) 'I've really tried, but I can't work out how to break down what I do into basic steps. Now I'm on my way and Roz thinks I'm ready to teach her.'

Eric replied instantly, 'You had enough faith to get in the car and drive. Trust in yourself a little more.'

Eric's voice was coming from the passenger seat. I couldn't see him clearly, just a shadowy outline. I kept my eye on the road. The trees were just beginning to bud.

'Is it going to be okay? I've no idea what I'm going to do.'

'I wouldn't be helping you if I mapped it out. You're going to learn as much from this in your own way as Roz will in hers.'

This was typical of Eric. Once again I felt envious of those mediums who say they get all their information, whatever they ask, from their guides. Eric would have none of that. He would steer me in the right direction – giving me clues with images or feelings, but never the answer. He always taught me that I had to look for myself and use my own mind.

Roz

Waiting for Mia to arrive, I realized I had no idea how we were going to work. Would there be formal classes? Would I have to write things down? Were there books I would have to read? Would she set me homework?

I got out my notebook and went through a checklist of Mia's predictions. Her vision of me in Wellington boots looking at chickens had never materialized – at least not yet. But my fridge-freezer had broken just as she said. One morning I found a pool of water on the kitchen floor and the door, hanging open, was 'wonky' and wouldn't close.

Then, unexpectedly, my brother offered to help me buy a new computer. Even more strange – for Christmas, my boyfriend, Mark, gave me a pair of stout new top-of-the-range walking boots.

Mia

The first thing I noticed when I stepped inside Roz's cottage was that it had a good atmosphere. The energy felt light and creative. It also felt homely. I wasn't expecting to be fed but, after making me a cup of tea, Roz set about cooking pasta for a late lunch. The house was as I had imagined it: cluttered with intriguing things. Chairs piled with papers. Books propped against the skirting boards. I was especially drawn to the Indian hangings on the walls.

After lunch, Roz put cushions on the front step so we could sit down. We looked out over the Mendip Hills. The last of the Spring sun was shining and I felt more relaxed than I had in a long time. The silence was soothing.

'I'm not sure what you're expecting, but I haven't got these lessons set in stone or written down. I've never done this before, so I've got to learn to teach you just as you've got to learn what I'm teaching you.'

'I'm trusting my instinct here – I've got a feeling about some people I want you to meet. An Australian couple have just arrived in England to see me and they are coming to Bath tomorrow. I think it would be a good idea for you to observe the meeting. They lost their daughter in the Bali bombing.'

Roz

I thought back to the newspaper reports of the nightclub bomb – over 200 young people had been killed while they were out partying.

Mia

'The couple are called Robert and Louise. I'll ask them if you can sit in. I think it's important for you to come because so much of being a psychic is about being able to be with other people's pain. Whatever the way someone dies, the suffering and loss for loved ones is universal. Bereavement is often the reason people seek the counsel of a psychic – or a priest or doctor. I consider these meetings the most important work I do.'

Roz

'They're coming all the way from Australia to meet you?'

Mia

'They read *The Gift* and the account of my son Shane's death: how I coped with the loss, it really struck a chord. They first contacted me six months ago. They told me about their daughter and said how much the book had touched them. I know what it's like to lose a child and feel desperate, so I emailed back my telephone number. Two days later, they called.

'We were on the phone for half an hour – it was a simple connection from one bereaved parent to another; nothing psychic. Later that day they emailed again saying they wanted to travel to see me. I tried to put them off – I said it was ridiculous to travel half way around the world to speak to me. I explained that I couldn't guarantee their daughter would come through to me, especially as she had only been dead a year. I wanted to protect them from themselves – from all that expense and huge expectation. But they insisted, they said they were coming to England.'

'Anyway, after all that driving I'm afraid I'm exhausted now. If it's okay with Robert and Louise, I'll pick you up in the morning and we'll go and meet them.'

* * *

Robert and Louise were more than happy for Roz to come along, so the next day we drove to Bath. On the way, I gave myself a pep talk. I still felt anxious at the thought that they had travelled a great distance and I might not be able to give them what they most wanted.

But no matter how much I wanted to help them, I knew I could only give them psychic information if I was absolutely sure of it. When Shane died, many so-called psychics telephoned me saying they had news of him from the other side. Not one of their so-called messages made any sense to me. I would hate to do that to someone else.

The moment I saw Robert and Louise standing at the entrance to the hotel, all my worries disappeared. I was filled with a feeling of love for them. They thanked me again for taking the time to see me – even though they were the ones who had travelled thousands of miles.

Since *The Gift* was published, a lot of people have started treating me as if I'm something special – as if I'm somehow different from them. But I am an ordinary person who drinks, swears and eats junk food. I'm not a saint. It's just that I have an ability to feel and see other people's lives – an ability that is lying dormant in all of us.

Roz

In the hotel lounge, we sat in an array of chairs and couches which we pulled together to make a circle.

Robert said, 'Within twenty minutes of reading *The Gift*, we made the decision to come to England to see you. We've read a lot of books since our daughter died, but what really grabbed us about your book was that you have actually experienced what we're going through. Your honesty made us feel an instant rapport with you.'

Mia

This was what it was all about. I was filled with strength and warmth at the thought of helping them.

Roz

Louise said, 'We were so nervous about phoning you, we kept passing the phone to each other, deciding who was going to make the call. I can't believe we are here now, on the other side of the world, talking to you.'

Louise took a large photograph album out of a carrier bag.

'This is Anne,' she said.

Mia

I looked at the photographs of a girl surrounded by family and friends. She was beautiful. My first psychic thought was the difference – as always – between the eyes of the living and the dead. When somebody is dead, the eyes in their photographs become flat; there seems to be no light behind them.

Showing me the pictures, Robert and Louise were hoping I'd be able to pick up some information about Anne. But I knew, instantly, that I wouldn't be able to do it. It was only a year since the bombing – too soon after her death for her to be able to come back and make contact. (Mostly, people return after a couple of years have passed and they have adjusted to being spirit.)

Robert and Louise's need, too, was getting in the way. Before I begin a reading, I usually ask people not to tell me anything about themselves. I already knew too much about Robert and Louise: how desperate they were, how far they had travelled. I found it hard to be impassive. I could not get into the zone.

I broke the meeting to go to the toilet. Standing inside the cubicle, I called Eric.

'Please give me a symbol, one thing about their daughter – just one thing to give them.'

I saw him smiling, telling me if I couldn't do it on my own, it wasn't the right time to do it. Knowing there would be no direct contact with their daughter, I went back in to the lounge to try to help Robert and Louise.

Roz

'Do you think it was her time to die?' Robert asked as soon as Mia sat down.

Mia

'Absolutely. Before you come to earth, it is already pre-destined how long you are going to be here. The time you die cannot be changed. I've known many instances where people have miraculously escaped death from horrific situations only to die a few days later in some bizarre way. The person missed their time and it's as if, from the other side, an emergency plan is made to bring them "home". We think our lives here are "home", but in truth "home" is on the other side.'

Roz

Robert said, 'I've got two questions. I've been carrying them around inside since Anne died.'

He spoke slowly, trying to hide his desperation.

'Is Anne okay?'

I watched him twist and untwist his hands.

'And will I see her again?'

Mia

'The biggest gift I've ever been given is the absolute knowledge of life after death. My greatest frustration is trying to find a way to convey that certainty to others.'

'I can categorically say that Anne is fine. In all my years of contact with spirit, I have never come across one that was distressed or afraid. And, yes, of course you are going to see her again.'

'Let me tell you how it works. When somebody dies, it is as if they are put into a drugged sleep and are very slowly awakened. This way, the shock of their death and the wrench of leaving those they love is accepted in a very gradual, serene way.'

'Years after my brother Pete died, he came back to tell me what it was like when he passed over. He told me he woke in the back of an ambulance and, as he sat up, he noticed a small man sitting opposite. The man was smiling at him, so Pete smiled back and said, "Alright?"'

'The man said, "I'm fine, and so are you. You are dead and it's time to come with me."'

'Pete told me, "You know the funny thing is, Mia, you would have thought I'd have freaked out. But I didn't. It didn't seem like a big deal at all. I just went with him."'

'The dead are always met by somebody, then once fully awakened on the other side, they benefit from the knowledge that they are going to see their family and friends again. Most of us on Earth haven't got the comfort of that knowledge. The decades that you live on after Anne's death seem an eternity to you but, for her, it is like the blink of an eye.'

'When Pete came back after he had been dead for a few years, he was still the mischievous, easy-going guy he'd been at the time of his death. At first, I was shocked. We think that the dead all turn into spiritual, holy beings. But their personalities don't change.'

'I want you to know that the person you know and love is exactly the same in spirit. When you see Anne again, she will be the person you know.'

Roz

Louise said, 'Since we lost Anne, we can't find a reason for anything. What's the point in working? What are we working for?'

Mia

'In decades to come, you're going to meet Anne and she will say to you, "Tell me what else you did, what adventures you had, what challenges you faced, whose lives you touched." Do you really want to blame her for the fact you gave up and wasted the rest of your life? You're not here by chance and you weren't born only to be a parent.'

'Life is school. The whole reason you are here is to learn. And the only way you learn is through emotional experiences.'

As we said goodbye in the hotel lobby, we arranged to meet again.

'I know your pain is immense, but it is not all that there is or will be. Even if you can't see it now, you will be able to understand it as time goes on.'

Although I do not usually hug clients, I embraced Robert and Louise.

'I look forward to seeing you again before you go back to Australia.'

Roz

Driving home with Mia, my mind was filled with Robert and Louise. Their grief was enormous. Even though she hadn't been able to make contact with Anne, Mia had reassured them that she was okay and that they would meet again. At the end of it, they seemed soothed, softened. How had she helped them? What was it that she had done?

She was a bereaved parent – she was able to connect with them, parent to parent. But she had some other quality – she allowed deep emotions to be expressed. She was not embarrassed by big feelings; on the contrary, she was matter of fact.

Robert and Louise had been at their most vulnerable and exposed. I had never seen people so raw. They had opened up so much. Mia clearly had something, but what was it? She seemed to have the ability to make people feel it was alright to be vulnerable – to be seen as they really were.

I asked her, 'Were you disappointed you didn't contact Anne?'

Mia

'It would have been nice to have received a message from Anne but that's not what it's about. The important thing is to be able to touch others at the deepest moments in their lives. To comfort them and give them a reason to carry on.

'I don't just see today. I see yesterday, today and tomorrow. The absolute thing we can all guarantee is that nothing stays the same. Luckily, that includes pain. My job is to help people to understand the bigger picture.'

Chapter 2

Need

Mia

I woke the next morning with a very clear idea of where we needed to go next. I telephoned Roz.

'The local spiritualist church will be a good place for our next lesson. Before I even begin teaching you to develop your sixth sense, I want you to get an idea of what this work is all about.'

Roz

As Mia drove to the spiritualist church in Bath, I sat beside her, imagining a room full of people speaking in tongues.

'What sort of people go to spiritualist churches?'

Mia

'I remember feeling worried the first time I went, but you'll be surprised. I want to show you the diversity of people in need.'

Roz

Bath First Spiritualist Centre was behind a plain door in a back street in the centre of the city. The only sign of activity was a man smoking a cigarette in the doorway. We paid £1.50 for entrance and were given a hymn book and raffle ticket and were told, 'The raffle will be drawn at the end of the service.'

We walked into the small hall. There were about 30 people in the congregation, sitting on wooden chairs in rows. The front of the hall was dominated by a modern-looking pulpit on a stage. Behind it were two ornately carved chairs on which sat a middle-aged woman and a dapper-looking older man in a suit.

People were clutching their hymn books and talking in hushed voices. I looked around. There was a girl in ripped jeans and a T-shirt; she had lots of piercings and her mobile phone kept going off. There was a woman in a tweed skirt, a twin-set and pearls. An old lady came in slowly with the aid of two sticks. Behind her, was a young man with a beard. He looked as if he had the weight of the world on his shoulders.

Many appeared troubled. Others looked as if they were fitting the meeting in with their shopping trip. On the stage, the man stood up. He had blue eyes and a gentle, continual smile.

'I'm Stan – as most of you know. Thank you all for coming. I'd like to ask you to turn your mobile phones off. We're happy to have Isla to take the service today. But let's start with the opening hymn.'

As we sang *Amazing Grace* to taped background music, I felt uncomfortable. I had a sense that most of us just wanted to get on with the mediumship and were putting up with the hymn singing to get to that.

The woman on the stage, introduced as 'today's medium', stood up. She was in her mid-fifties and was wearing a neat blue skirt and matching cardigan. She gave the address, reading a passage of Native American spiritual philosophy. Half way through the words about the higher self and the power of thought, she lost me. By the looks on their faces, I could see that most people in the room had similarly lost the thread. Isla seemed nervous and poured herself a drink of water.

'If I come to talk to you, please acknowledge me verbally to make the connection. If you don't understand the information

I'm giving you, don't disregard it, your understanding of it may come later.'

The atmosphere changed. I could feel the charge of expectation; the excitement in the room was contagious.

She pointed at the old woman with walking sticks, wearing a red cardigan.

'I'd like to come to the lady in red,' Isla said.

The woman had obviously been to quite a few of these meetings as she smiled and said 'Thank you,' quite comfortably. Isla went on to tell her that she could see a man in spirit standing near her, who loved to garden and was worried about her spending too much time on her own.

'The man just wants to say that he visits often and is looking over you.'

In this vein, Isla continued to go to different members of the audience. At least three people received the same message: that they were worried or had been under stress, but there was a lot of love around them from spirit and it was going to get better. The only difference was in the flowers given as loving symbols at the end of each mini reading. Some got carnations, others lilies or roses 'in a spray'.

After about an hour, the medium asked us to join her for the closing prayer. I realized suddenly that this was all we were going to get. I felt dissatisfied, and wondered how many other people there felt the same. I was amazed when I saw people queuing up to thank her.

Gathering my bag and coat, I was stopped by the announcement that the raffle was about to be drawn. A woman won a picture frame. A man got a tin of sweets. For the final prize, Stan thrust the bowl of raffle tickets in my face.

'Would you like to pick out the last ticket?' he asked.

As I looked at the folded slips of paper, I knew which one I wanted to choose. I pulled it out and looked at the number. I

21

was instantly embarrassed.

'It's my number.'

I tried to put it back, but Stan was insistent.

'You take the prize,' he said, handing me a photograph album adorned with kittens. 'You're obviously psychic.'

Outside the church Mia, still chuckling, lit up a cigarette.

Mia

'Well, you used your instincts well there, Roz, choosing the winning ticket.'

Roz

'It was just a coincidence.'

Mia

'Coincidences are more than they seem. They are doorways to the bigger picture. Everything is interconnected and coincidences show you that you are in tune with the invisible web.'

'If you could look through a special lens, you would see millions of strands of energy connecting everyone. These strands also link action and consequence. Something you do today will affect someone, somewhere, at some time. Coincidences are part of the web. They remind you to be in tune with the consequences of your actions. Coincidences are the helping hand of destiny – nudges to keep you on your path.'

'Anyway, what did you think of the session?'

Roz

'I wasn't very impressed by the medium.'

Mia

'For some of the people there, maybe it was enough that she was acknowledging their loss.'

Roz

'She didn't go far enough. If she'd spent a bit longer with each person, maybe she would have given them something more tangible. Her messages seemed pretty superficial to me. I wanted to be wowed.'

Mia

'That wasn't the reason I took you.'

Roz

We wandered into Abbey Square and sat on a bench, looking up at the old, stone walls.

Mia

'What was your first impression when you went in the spiritualist church? Do you remember the atmosphere?'

Roz

'I remember feeling awkward.'

Mia

'Do you think anyone else felt like that?'

Roz

'A few did. I remember looking round. I felt a bit uncomfortable about singing the hymn, too.'

Mia

'So did a lot of other people there. And the talk seemed to go over most people's heads – including mine. But when the medium started to say, "If I come to you acknowledge me", and we knew she was about to start the mediumship, did you feel the change in the atmosphere?'

Roz

'Yes, there was an undercurrent of expectation, excitement and need.'

Mia

'That's what I wanted to show you. It didn't matter what the medium said, or how good her information was, it was the *need* that I wanted you to be aware of.'

Roz

We sat in silence, watching the pigeons and a busker with a guitar. I'd thought Mia might start our lessons by dazzling me with visions. Instead, she was showing me the human face of her work: people's vulnerability and loss, feelings that are usually covered up.

Mia

'The need you saw is universal. It is my hope that, at the end of our time together, when you're faced with this need in someone, you'll know what to do.'

Roz

In the spiritualist church – as with Robert and Louise – I'd been moved by people's need for information about their dead loved ones, their longing for the comfort of knowing that death is not the end. Their need for reassurance was huge, and yet Mia was telling me that in six months time I was actually going to be of benefit.

'I'm not sure I'll ever have the skills to be useful to people in that much pain and need.'

Mia

'I've shown you the end result, but when I come next time we'll go back to the very beginning. There's more in the world than your eyes can see – sights and colours that you have never experienced. It's as if all your life you have been seeing in black and white and I am going to give you colour vision. I'm going to take you on a journey. I'm going to change the way you see forever.'

Chapter 3

—⚬—

Life Energy

Mia

The night before my second visit to Roz, I couldn't sleep. The last time we'd been together, I'd used a lot of grand words, but the nitty-gritty of how to share my knowledge still eluded me. Teaching someone to find and use their sixth sense was very different from my own experience of becoming psychic. For me it had never been a choice. The gift was thrust on me.

Twenty years on, it was a gift not a curse, but how was I going to teach all this to Roz? I decided to open up and find Eric. I got into a comfortable position and stopped all thoughts to clear my mind.

'Eric.'

Immediately, his face was clear in my head.

'I'm really stressed about teaching Roz. Why did I offer to give up my time and put myself under this pressure? What am I trying to prove?'

I was giving him all my angst – the truth of how inadequate and overwhelmed I felt. I finished with the biggest question of all:

'Why am I so negative about myself?'

'Let's start with all the things you think are bad about yourself,' Eric said.

He looked at me patiently.

'That's easy. I'm lazy, I'm selfish, I eat too much, I smoke too much, I don't see things through, I don't look after myself properly …'

The list seemed endless. I was still grumbling about my faults, when Eric said, 'Now tell me the good things about yourself.'

My mind went blank. I couldn't think of a single thing.

'I like to help people if they're feeling bad,' I said at last.

That felt like a good thing. What else?

'I think I've got quite nice eyes,' I sputtered weakly.

'And is that it?' Eric asked gently.

I thought really hard. I still couldn't think of another thing I liked about myself.

'Yes,' I said. 'That's it. It's bad, isn't it?'

'It's not great,' Eric admitted, 'but if the list was the other way around it would get in the way of you helping others. The problem is the lack of balance.'

As he spoke, I had a vision of a piece of paper with a long list of faults on one side and two words – my good points – on the other. It was a revelation. I knew this list was about self worth and I was being shown, vividly, how low my self-esteem was. But, even with that knowledge, I still couldn't find another plus point to balance out my list.

I had never realized before quite how low my self-image was. Becoming a 'teacher' – someone with knowledge to impart – was bringing all my doubts to the surface. It was a shock to see that, although I liked almost everybody I came across, I didn't like myself very much at all.

'How is this information meant to help me then, Eric?' I asked. 'It's giving me even more to worry about.'

'The one thing that has never changed is your belief in helping other people,' Eric said. 'It is part of who you are. It's the one thing that even you can't deny yourself.'

It was true. No matter how much I put myself down, the desire to help others has always been a part of me. I recalled my earliest memory: there I was, aged three, standing at the doorway to my home, watching the other children playing and feeling a great urge to look after them. Nothing could rock that.

'By teaching Roz, you are going to help her,' Eric said. 'You have natural compassion, trust that.'

With the comfort of thinking that I might actually benefit Roz, I drifted off to sleep.

* * *

Roz

The night before Mia's second visit, I couldn't sleep. I felt excited, anxious to get going and start seeing things. At the same time, I couldn't stop thinking about the film *The Exorcist*. I hoped my lessons with Mia would not involve my head spinning round while I vomited. What was I inviting in?

I had been a journalist for 20 years; my scepticism kept me grounded. So why was I feeling so unsure, so afraid? When Mia arrived, I quizzed her nervously.

'This is quite safe, isn't it? I'm not going to get stuck with a ghost, am I?'

Mia

'Don't worry, you're totally safe. It's very unusual to be able to find a ghost – let alone be stuck with one. I've come across haunted places and buildings, but never a person. It doesn't work like that. If you are lucky enough to have contact with a ghost, I promise you it won't be interested in scaring you. It will merely want to communicate.'

'Ghosts are often visitors – they come back to see a person or place that was important to them when they were alive. The ghosts I speak to during the course of a reading are visitors. They are aware of their death and only come back for a short time.'

'Many ghosts, however, don't even realize they are dead. They are earthbound spirits, commonly known as "hauntings". At the moment they died, the powerful emotions of anger or distress were so overwhelming, they refused to accept their death and go "home". To them, this emotion is unresolved business. And a spirit cannot be forced home. It has to go willingly.'

'There is a third kind of "ghost". Here, the moment of death causes such a strong emotional outpouring that it leaves a residue or imprint of the event in the place that it occurred. There is no actual spirit presence, but instead the earth becomes a kind of tape recorder and the event replays itself over and over. In this instance, people might see, for example, a grey lady appearing on the same staircase at the same time on the same day each year.'

'For us, the idea of being in spirit form, stuck on Earth where nobody can see us, sounds desperately lonely. But the reality is that ghosts are never distressed. They are just a bit confused. Even if I say, "You're not meant to be here, you're dead" – as I used to do in the beginning – they don't take any notice.'

'I remember one of the first hauntings I went to. I was called to a country cottage where the ghost of a young woman had been seen repeatedly. When I went upstairs, I saw a woman of about thirty standing in the middle of a bedroom. She was looking towards a window with a dreamy expression on her face.'

'I said, "Hello", and she smiled gently. There was no big emotion there.'

'I said something stupid like, "Are you stuck here?"'

'She totally ignored me and wandered towards the window and looked out. I stood beside her at the window thinking: say something, Mia, you have to get the contact going. So I said, "It's a lovely garden isn't it?"'

'She looked at me, all animated and said, "Yes, isn't it?"'

'I tried again. "Do you know you're dead?" I asked gently, but she simply pointed to the roses in the garden. I realized she was happy to talk about her surroundings, as if this was still her home but any reference to the fact she was spirit was totally dismissed. It was as if she – and all Earth-bound spirits – have a safety valve which protects them from any painful emotion.'

'It was only when Eric came in and held her hand that she seemed to acknowledge her death and she went over with him. Since then I've learned that it would be dangerous or upsetting for somebody like myself to awaken the knowledge they are dead without the presence of a spirit guide to take them over once they know.'

'You're a long way from making contact with ghosts, so calm down. We are only going to look at auras today.'

Roz

Mia's answer was reassuring. We were not going to get into anything spooky and her presence was so earthy, I felt my stomach begin to unclench.

'So what is an aura?'

Mia

'Every living thing has a life force. Think of it as electricity. It is an energy and this energy fills every part of your body.'

Floundering slightly at having to explain what I knew instinctively, I called Eric.

'How can I explain an aura?'

In the beginning, when I spoke to Eric he would often say things that didn't make any sense to me. He would then show me a picture in my mind to help me understand what he was trying to explain. Very quickly, we developed a communication where pictures came as fast as words.

Now he showed me a room with a large fire. Then the door shut and, even though I couldn't see the fire, I could still feel the heat radiating from the room. I gave this image to Roz but she was still looking puzzled, so I explained, 'Just as the room can't contain all that heat, so your life force is inside your body but your body can't hold all of it. Your life force radiates around the edges. This over-spill is your aura.'

'The more complex the being, the more complex the life force. Years ago, I had this all explained to me when I was ill in hospital. I was drifting in and out of consciousness when the spirit of my dead brother, Pete, appeared beside me and placed a large leather-bound book in my hands.'

'"Open the book," he said.'

'The first pictures I saw were of the sea and the minute organisms that lived there. In each of these organisms – amoeba, plankton, seaweed – there was a tiny flicker of light. Just one.'

'Then I saw small fish go by; each of them had two or three lines of flickering light. The important thing, the book told me, was to see the life force in everything. I was shown a rain forest filled with huge trees. Each tree had three or four strong lines of light moving through the trunk. At the canopy, the leaves had wonderful, soft flickers of light moving through their veins.'

'I saw the forest floor and a formation of ants moving over the trunk of a fallen tree. I marvelled at the beauty of the lights in their bodies. The book went on to show me reptiles, birds and animals, all with increasing amounts of light.'

'The last picture was of a city, full of human beings. I saw the intricacy of millions of moving lines of light that make up the human form. Layer upon layer of tiny white pulsating lines. The same light was in the amoeba and in the human. What differed was the complexity and amount of light in each.'

Roz

'Why can't everyone see these lights?'

Mia

'Because they don't know how to look.'

Roz

I thought of the wildlife programmes on TV that are able to show night-vision scenes. Even in the pitch black, special thermal cameras can detect animals from their body heat and film them in amazing detail. Without the special lens, the viewer would not be able to see anything. But that didn't mean it wasn't there.

'Is it like finding a special lens?'

Mia

'In a way, but you find the lens inside of you.'

'Even if you don't believe in auras, just be open-minded enough to try to see what' s there. Don't let prejudice cover your sight. If you are determined not to see, then you won't.'

'I am going to move about six feet away so that you have the space that's needed to see. Now focus six inches above my head. Relax. Slightly unfocus your eyes and try not to blink.'

Roz

'I can't see anything.'

Mia

I moved away from the bookcase to sit in front of a white wall. Then I slightly lowered the lighting by switching off a lamp.

'Seeing auras always works better if there is a plain background. You need to be able to see clearly, but it's best if the light is not too bright.'

Roz

'I still can't see anything.'

Mia

'Of course you can't see anything, you've only just started. It's important not to be emotionally involved. You mustn't care what you see. Don't expect to see anything. Just wait.'

Roz

I tried to feel nonchalant and carried on looking. And looking.

Suddenly I caught sight of a hazy white shadow pulsing around Mia's head. I focused on the shadow – and lost it.

'I think I saw an uneven glow around your head. It was like the oil in a lava lamp, moving and changing all the time. Was that it?'

Mia

'Yes. Well done. The first time you see any aura, you will see it as either white or gold. This is not a person's aura colours, it is just the first stage of sight. Try again.'

Roz

I was excited. This was going to be easy. I refocused on the spot above Mia's head. Nothing happened. I couldn't see the light I'd seen before. I felt disappointed. Had I really seen it the first time?

'I can't do it now. It's gone.'

Mia

'It's not gone, Roz. The first time you didn't know what to expect. You were impassive. That's why it came easily. But once you'd seen it, you knew what you were looking for and that got in the way.'

'Settle down, try to feel non-emotional and just see what is, not what you expect there to be.'

Roz

This was easier said than done but, just as I was about to give up, I saw the white shadow around Mia again.

'It's bigger this time. Thicker.'

Mia

'The more you get used to seeing auras, the more you will see. As you get more proficient, you may start to see colours in auras. Alternatively, you may only ever see white but flashes of colour may come in your mind.'

Roz

'Can you see my aura?'

Mia

'As I first focus on you, from your head to your shoulders, I see white, eight inches deep.'

Roz

'That's much wider than the light I saw around your head.'

Mia

'When I started, the auras I saw were probably only an inch wide. As I said, the more you look, the more you see.'

'The white is like a mist and it is filling up with blue. There is light blue above your head. Around the sides is a mixture of greens, brown and pink. Light blue means you are a people person, you care for others.'

'Green is a practical colour. It means you are going to be caught up in the practical necessities of life. Brown is earth, it means you're grounded. Pink is stress. Don't worry, everyone has a certain amount of pink.'

'What's really interesting is you have a strong purple colour weaving through the rest, which indicates a healer or carer of souls.'

Roz

Mia was looking to the right – as if someone was standing there and talking to her. Eric – or whatever it was – was holding her total attention.

'Is Eric in the room?'

Mia

'He's sitting in that wicker chair but, as I look, it's not actually your chair. He's sitting in an old brown leather chair, in the same place as your wicker one. Are you okay with that?'

Roz

'I'm not sure I believe it, actually.'

Mia

'That's okay.'

* * *

Roz

After Mia had left to go to the B&B, I sat for a while in my living room. The idea of Mia talking to her spirit guide didn't scare me, but I was disappointed that I didn't have a sense of him myself. If Eric was really there, wouldn't I have felt his presence? Alone now, I tried to sense any change in the room, but it felt the same as always. Did Mia's guide leave the room when she did?

It felt disloyal, but I couldn't help wondering whether Eric was real – or whether he was a part of Mia. I believe we all have a higher self – a spark that makes us want to be our best self.

Perhaps – consciously or unconsciously – Mia was giving that part of herself a character and a name.

I wondered if what she would be teaching me would be ways to have more contact with my higher self. One way or another, the journey had begun.

Chapter 4

—⚬—

Magic

Roz

The next morning, Mia took me to Bath to people-watch. As a writer, looking at other people is one of my favourite pastimes, but today, Mia said, I would be looking in a different way.

Mia

'When I first discovered I could see auras, my children were at school and I used my time to play. I used to sit in cafés, looking at people's auras. I loved my new ability to see people glowing.'

'I remember one morning seeing a woman smiling to herself as she stirred her tea. Curiosity aroused, I made eye contact, then looked away. I realized she had just found out she was pregnant. Her aura was filled with gold. Happiness shows like champagne bubbles. They don't last for long, but they are always good to see.'

'Twenty years on, I haven't lost the initial wonderment at seeing people's auras. I want to see if you can do the same thing.'

Roz

We parked the car and walked through the winding streets of Bath, peering in café windows, looking for signs of busyness – our unwitting psychic subjects. At last, we found a café with people clustered around circular tables. We positioned ourselves in a corner and ordered breakfast with large coffees.

At the table directly in front of us, there was a woman with tousled blonde hair. I focused six inches above her head, held my gaze steady and tried to see her aura. Nothing. I looked across the room at a man in the corner, reading a newspaper. Again, I tried to see his aura and again, I saw nothing at all. I had lost the ability to see.

'I can't do it, I can't see anything.'

Mia

'You tried to start already? We just walked a mile looking at cafés, you're cold, your heart is still pumping, you haven't even taken your jacket off. You're not comfortable enough to see anything.'

Roz

I realized I was expecting a lot of myself – I wanted instant results.

'So what should I do?'

Mia

'You haven't got to be in a state of meditation, but you do have to be comfortable. If your body is uncomfortable in any way, it calls your attention away. Over the years, I have tried many different ways to relax. For me, the important thing is that relaxation is instant – like changing the station on a radio. If I asked you to clench a muscle, you could do it easily – I believe it is just as easy to let it go.'

'The best and quickest way I've found – and the one I use before every reading – is the "sigh and drop" routine. Sit comfortably and put your hands in a relaxed position – it doesn't matter where you place them as long as they are not tight or clenched.'

'Lots of people say focus on your breath and breathe deeply, but I find one big sigh is enough. Take a deep breath in and hold it for a moment. Then, as you sigh and the air comes out of your lungs, let everything – all the muscles in your body – drop. Shoulders, back, hips, stomach, chest, thighs. Let them all go.'

'Suddenly you will be able to feel the weight of your body in the chair. You have just brought yourself back to you.'

Roz

I always thought relaxation involved focused breathing but this 'dropping' into a relaxed state was surprisingly effective – and quick. I looked again at the table in front of us. The blonde woman was eating chips. I focused my eyes above her head and suddenly it was there – two inches of shimmering white light haloing her shoulders and head.

In a city café, I was looking at a stranger and seeing her aura. It was incredibly exciting – could it be for real?

'See the woman at the next table. I managed to see her aura but I could only see it for a couple of seconds and then it was gone.'

Mia

Looking at the light in Roz's eyes, I could see her excitement. And I was sharing it. Our first trip out and she was seeing auras in an every day situation – it was more than I had expected.

'Great. Now try someone else.'

Roz

I looked around the café, trying to appear inconspicuous. To my left, a man sat reading a book. I tried to see his aura, but couldn't.

'I'm trying to see that man's aura over there, and I can't get it.'

Mia

'That's because he's sitting in front of a poster – there's too much information in the background. Your eyes are having to deal with all those colours; they're not being allowed to rest.'

'Very early on, I discovered that if there was a plain background it was much easier to see. If there's a busy background, you have to work harder to see a person's aura.'

Roz

I looked back at the blonde-haired woman. She was sitting in front of a white wall, but now she had been joined by an older woman. I tried to see her aura again but, although I caught glimpses of it, it was harder to see than before. Exasperated, I wondered if my ability to see auras had been a fluke.

'I'm not sure if I'm seeing auras or not. I'm looking at the same woman, but I'm only getting flashes of white around her. It's not constant.'

Mia

'Okay, what's changed since the last time you looked?'

Roz

'Nothing apart from the fact that she's talking.'

Mia

'That's it, Roz. She's not as still as the first time you looked. The faster somebody is moving, the harder it is to see their aura. To get your confidence back, do the sigh and drop routine and then look at that guy sitting on his own in the corner.'

Roz

He was drinking a cup of tea and staring out of the window. As I focused above his head, I saw the white light around him.

'I've got it, but how do I know it's real? How do I know I'm not making it up?'

Mia

'Okay, look at the till and find its aura.'

Roz

I swivelled round in my chair and looked a few inches above the till. Nothing. No matter how hard I tried, I couldn't get any signs of light around this mechanical device. It was reassuring. I couldn't put an aura there just because I wanted to.

Mia

'Now look at that plant.'

Roz

A few feet away, there was a large pot plant trailing masses of small leaves.

'I'm focusing above it, but I can't see anything.'

Mia

I sat for a minute or two, looking at the plant and seeing its aura. How was I seeing it? This was something I had never questioned. It came so naturally to me. Then I realized I was looking at the plant, not above it.

'Okay, Roz, because the plant is so still and has a much smaller life force, you need to look directly at it. Look at one leaf and slightly unfocus your eyes. Remember, just look don't expect anything.'

Roz

Looking at one leaf, I tried not to blink. Suddenly I saw a thin white light, edging the whole leaf. It was much more symmetrical than the other auras I had seen.

'I've got it.'

I was amazed.

'So plants really do have auras?'

Mia

'Every living thing has an aura. But as you've seen, every aura is different. If we hadn't practised last night, then it would have been very difficult for you to see auras today. Today a little bit of you already believed you could see and that belief helped you.'

'One of the very first conversations I had with Eric was about the word "belief". When I was struggling to tame my gift, he explained, "The power of belief is like a magic key, for the more you believe in something, the more possible that something becomes. When beginning your journey into psychic awareness, try to believe that it is possible. And, as your abilities grow, so too will your belief."'

* * *

Roz

After Mia dropped me off at home, I decided to go for a walk. It was a light spring evening and the first crocuses edged the footpath out towards the fields. As I walked, I had a feeling of hopefulness. I had seen my first auras.

The great thing about being with Mia was that she was continually reinforcing the idea that I could trust my instincts. Again, I wondered if seeing the energy around the people in the café had been my imagination. But even if it was, it lead to a feeling of respect for them, and wonder. That in itself felt worthwhile. If more people did that, I reflected, then we would live in a much gentler world. For how could you want to kill someone if you were tuning into their energy?

Was I being gullible? I dug my hands into my jacket pockets. Was I deluding myself? Mia kept saying that belief was the key, but if I was going to believe in something, then I wanted to be sure it was something that actually existed.

I turned towards home. By the stables, a large marmalade cat started walking purposefully towards me. I adore cats and always stop to stroke them. This one was unusually friendly and rolled over on its back in the dust, stretching out its paws.

As I walked away, the cat started to follow me. I looked at it against the dark green bushes and, suddenly, I could see a white light along its back. The light was neither transparent nor dense. I looked away and then back. The light was still there. I was seeing its aura. I shook my head in wonderment. Mia – the powerhouse – was gone, but even without her presence, the magic remained.

* * *

Sitting on the front step of my cottage the next morning, I watched my cat, Wesley, sprawling in the long grass. He was lying quite still and the backdrop of green grass was uniform and plain.

Oh my god – there it was. My cat was glowing. I looked away, thinking, as always, that I could be making it up. I glanced back and the pulsating line was still there. Perhaps Mia was right and everything had an aura. I felt a knot in my stomach. I wanted and didn't want to see it, all at the same time.

Plant pot. I looked at the empty terracotta plant pot at the bottom of the steps. I tried to make it have an aura; I scrunched my eyes up and played with the morning light. It was like the cash till in the café. There was no aura to be found.

I was seeing stuff that I had never seen before – and I could see it at will. Had something changed in me? Could I go back to the way I was before? Could I stop it if I wanted to?

Did taking on board the existence of auras, mean I had to believe in ghosts and the afterlife? Was it all part of the same package? Could I just choose the bits (the safe-feeling bits) that I wanted to take on, and leave the rest behind?

I reminded myself that Mia and I had only just started – and all I had promised was that I would keep an open mind. Then I let myself feel the excitement again, the wonder. Wesley was still glowing, so was the tree at the bottom of the garden. Mia had, indeed, given me a magic lens.

* * *

Mia

Driving back to see Roz two weeks later, I felt excited at finding out how she had progressed. She had seen something that most people think would be impossible to see – she had seen her first auras. I hoped too that her first feelings of belief had been stirred. I felt pleased with myself that I had found a way to teach her how to see.

I arrived at the cottage and Roz gave me a progress report – how she had seen first the marmalade cat's aura and then Wesley's. I was pleased, but also amazed at how quickly and easily she had taken the teaching on. I had confirmation: if you persevere, you *can* develop and use your sixth sense. Our journey seemed to be gathering a pace of its own.

'She's got it very quickly, hasn't she Eric?' I said when Roz was out of the room.

'She may have been sceptical but she has worked at being open-minded. And, at this point, that is all that is needed.'

'Is it always going to be this easy?' I asked.

'When you find the right words, there's no reason why not.'

With this, I knew Eric had no intention of giving me the right words but I felt comforted. Perhaps I did have the ability to be a teacher, after all.

Roz came back into the room with two steaming mugs of tea. I knew what we had to do next.

'Okay, you've seen auras, now I want you to do something different with this ability. Remember what I said, the aura is an energy – like heat, like the wind, like electricity. I wanted you to see it first so you know it is there. But now I want you to *feel* it.'

Roz was looking at me expectantly – as if I was indeed her teacher. I was getting caught up in her excitement, buzzing at the thought of sharing my world with her. I felt that I had spent 20 years telling people 'there is a magic kingdom' and now, for the first time, I was able to show someone my special place and share the wonder.

Out of the corner of my eye, I saw Eric sitting in his leather chair in Roz's living room. Since Eric had taught me how to be psychic, he had taken a lesser role in the work that I did. These days, he was just there as an advisor when I really needed him. The fact that he was in the room with us again, made me realize he was taking an active interest in these teachings.

I didn't bother mentioning Eric's presence to Roz. There was no need at this point. She had enough to deal with. She could get used to Eric slowly. There was no rush.

'Okay Roz, let's start with the sigh-and-drop routine. Settle yourself, make sure you're comfortable. As you sigh, let everything drop. Remember those muscles are just as easy to drop as to clench. Let them go. Now hold your hand out towards me with your palm down.'

I placed my hand, palm up, three to four inches below hers.

'Can you feel anything?'

Roz
'No.'

Mia
'The object of this exercise is to feel each other's auras. Move your hand slowly up and down a few inches, so you are going

away from my hand and then back towards it. You've seen auras and you know they exist. Up to now, you've only seen them around the head of a person, but actually the aura is around every part of your body. So your hand is radiating its aura and so is mine.'

'What we're trying to feel is when our two auras touch. There should be a very slight resistance.'

Roz
'Why a resistance?'

Mia
'Because it is two energies touching. If two winds come together, they form a tornado. If two electrical currents come together, they cause a spark. If two radio waves come together, they crackle. There is always a reaction when two energies meet.'

'Some people feel resistance as a warmth or tingling, some as a sensation of cold. There is no set reaction, no right or wrong way. Once again, be open-minded and wait to see what you feel. Don't expect anything.'

Roz
It took several goes – including another tea break – and then suddenly I felt a tingling in my palm. It was barely perceptible but, when I focused on it, I could feel that it was warm too. I had been holding my hand out for half an hour, so maybe it wasn't surprising that it was tingling. I moved my hand away from Mia's and the feeling went.

'I'm not sure whether I was imagining it or not. But I think I felt a tingling in my palm.'

Mia
'Try again.'

Roz

There it was, waiting for me. I moved my hand away and back, away and back. It was definitely only there when my hand was close to Mia's.

'Maybe it's just the heat of your body, I'm picking up.'

Mia

'Then why didn't you feel it for the first half hour? And why is it so much easier to feel now?'

Roz

'I don't know.'

I felt flustered.

'I can see a glow and I can feel something, but what does it mean? What's it for?'

Mia

'The real and constant you is energy. You can call it your spirit or your etheric body or your soul. What you have seen and felt is the proof that this energy exists. There would be no point in teaching you anything without that knowledge. It makes it easier for us to uncover your psychic abilities.'

* * *

Mia

Back at the B&B that night, I went to the bar and ordered a large vodka and tonic and took it up to my room with me. Since I'd asked the owners to pile two mattresses on top of each other to ease my bad back, my bed had become a haven and I collapsed into it, book, cigarettes, ashtray and vodka and tonic to hand.

I had just started unwinding, when I heard footsteps outside my bedroom door. Nothing unusual about that – there were two other bedrooms on the landing – but these footsteps went back and forth, back and forth. Eventually, I got up and opened the door. There was no one there. Peering into the darkness, I looked up and down the corridor. All was quiet. The footsteps had stopped.

I smiled to myself. Wherever I go, spirits appear. It stopped freaking me out a long time ago. I acknowledged the corridor-pacing spirit in my heart and went back to bed.

Spirits seem to know when I'm around. I remembered a night when a spirit got physical with me. I was out for dinner with friends and we were sitting at the bar waiting for a table when, suddenly, I was pushed so hard in the back that I flew off my stool and landed several feet away.

I played it down to my friends, pretending I had slipped (I didn't want to be talking about ghosts all evening) but when it happened again, I got angry. I stormed into the corridor and waited. It only took a couple of minutes for the spirit of a woman to appear in front of me. She was in her forties and wearing a tweed jacket and skirt.

'What the hell was that about?' I asked her.

'I've been trying to talk to you since you came in,' she said, 'but you wouldn't listen.'

'You didn't have to throw me across the bloody bar.'

'I'm sorry,' she said. 'I just wanted to get your attention.'

With that, my anger went. It took 15 minutes to send her home with Eric's help. Then I rejoined my friends at the bar and explained, 'Before you ask, yes, it was a ghost and, yes, I've sorted it. The woman wasn't bad, she was just trying to get my attention. She died twenty-five years ago and had been waiting a long time to go home.'

Lying in bed, my thoughts came back to teaching Roz. Awake now, my mind was buzzing. I realized there was an easier way to start feeling auras – Roz could feel her own. It was so simple. I could hardly wait to see her.

The next day, sitting in Roz's living room, I said, 'Sit in a comfortable position, Roz, and start with the sigh and drop routine. Breathe out and let all your muscles fall. I know I keep saying it, but it is as easy to let the muscles drop as it is to hold them in tension.

'Put the palms of your hands together in front of you, as if in prayer. Keep your fingers closed. Now move your hands four inches apart and hold that position. Stay relaxed. Can you feel anything?'

Roz
'I don't think so.'

Mia
'Slowly move your hands together, but don't let them touch. Now slowly move them back to four inches apart. Repeat it in a slow and constant movement. Remember to keep your fingers closed. Can you feel anything now?'

Roz
'As my hands get near to each other, I can feel a bit of heat. When I move my hands away again, it goes.'

Mia
'Okay, that's good. Now when you get to the position where you feel the heat, hold it.'

Roz
I held my hands an inch apart. The heat increased slightly.
    'Oh yes, I can feel heat. It's getting hotter.'
    Then it went.
    'It's gone.'

Mia

I looked over at Roz and saw that in her excitement she had become tense. Her shoulders were hunched, as if she was straining to feel.

'Roz, stay exactly as you are, but tell me, are your muscles relaxed? Tension creeps up on you – and you don't realize. One minute you are relaxed, the next you get interested and the excitement or concentration makes you bunch up. You need to keep a constant physical check on yourself.'

'Most people feel heat or tingling very quickly. If they don't, they're not relaxed enough. They just need to relax more.'

Roz

I sighed and dropped to relax. I tried to feel my aura again. I felt the heat much more quickly this time. And a bit of tingling too. I was definitely feeling something.

'I've got the heat back, but I've got tingling as well now.'

Mia

I could hear her excitement.

'Be impassive, just look, just see. Don't get excited. Let it be. It just is.'

Roz

I stopped and started a few times. I had a sense of wonder. This feeling was on tap.

'How come I've never felt this before?'

Mia

'Because you've never tried.'

Roz

'But this is amazing. People have prayed with their hands in a similar position for thousands of years, yet no one has mentioned this sensation. Why?'

Mia

'I don't know, let me ask Eric.'

'Eric, is there any significance between being able to feel your aura between your hands and the ancient position of prayer?'

'Yes,' he replied straight away. 'It is no coincidence that in some cultures the position of prayer and that of greeting uses this hand position. Thousands of years ago, people knew about this and that's why some of them started using their hands to pray. It is a way of acknowledging spirit within the body, an acceptance that we really are spirit. When you acknowledge it, the spiritual world isn't so far away.'

This made sense to me; like so much of Eric's information, once said, it always seemed so obvious.

Eric continued, 'When you acknowledge and feel your own spirit, then you have a direct link to God – or however you perceive God to be. It is like a magic bridge. It is a powerful position because first you feel your spirit between your hands and, with that sensation, your belief is ignited. With the power of that belief you cross the divide.'

What a simple and beautiful answer. I felt a sense of awe at learning this lost information. Thanks to Roz's questions, I was learning so much. I was always looking for ways to show people my world and comfort those I could not be with. Here was a new tool. Now others could feel the sense of unity that I felt when I prayed this way.

As if agreeing with me, Eric said, 'This simple technique of feeling and acknowledging your aura and then praying can be a powerful comforter to those in emotional or physical pain. A lot of people who are hurting feel they have to find someone to help them – a priest, a psychic, a counsellor or a doctor – because they feel so alone.'

'But they can help themselves. All they have to do is acknowledge their spiritual self, their etheric body, their soul – whatever name they wish to use. Then they will realize that they are not alone. All they have to do is ask and they will be comforted and guided. You don't have to be a brilliant psychic to have this gift. Just believe it and do it.'

As I heard Eric's voice fading, I realized that whenever I needed a stronger connection with God, I automatically went into the position of holding my hands in front of me, several inches apart. It was instinctive. It gave me an immediate, deep connection. Yet, until that moment, I had never realized its relevance.

Prayer can be off-putting – it seems too rule-bound, too structured – but I wanted Roz to know how natural, how useful it could be.

'When I pray, I talk to God like you would talk to a friend. I don't say set prayers. I just talk about how I'm feeling and ask for some help. It's like phoning your best mate who is on the other side of the world. Just having that communication is a balm in itself.'

'God is always listening. And when we feel most alone and abandoned, those are the times we learn our biggest lessons. When my son was dying, I prayed all through the night for God to spare him. I prayed so hard and for so long, I didn't doubt that my prayers would be answered. And then he died. My rage was enormous. I felt cheated and betrayed.'

'Now I understand that I was asking for something that couldn't be given. It was Shane's time to go. What I received was the strength to survive my loss. When we pray, we may not receive what we want, but we will always receive what we need.'

'I want to show you something else. Go back to the position where you can feel your aura. Remember to relax and keep your fingers closed. Now when you feel the heat or the tingling, hold that position and let it build. I'm going to show you how to play with your aura.'

'Very gently, move your hands a couple of inches away from each other and then back to the position where you can feel your aura. Do this again and again with soft, regular movements.'

'What you should feel is a resistance when your hands are nearest to each other. The more you do this, the more it will feel as if your hands are being bounced apart. Even though I have been playing with my aura like this for years, I still get satisfaction and pleasure from doing it. I refer to it as "bouncing my aura".'

Roz

Quite quickly, I could feel the bouncy sensation Mia was describing.

'I can feel the resistance. It is as if my hands had a small, light, spring between them.'

Mia

'Now sigh and drop, and try this. Put your index fingers half-an-inch apart in front of you, facing inwards. It doesn't matter what the rest of your hands are doing as long as they are comfortable. Look at the outline at the top of your fingers. Remember: just look, don't have any expectations. See what you can see.'

Roz

'I can see the aura around each finger. It seems to be thicker on the inside of my fingers.'

Mia

'Well done. As you get more used to doing this, you may see the aura around each finger expand to touch the next finger. You might also see what looks like smoke going between the fingers. But this is just your own energy attracting itself to itself. This is something you can practise by yourself. The more you do it, the easier it will be for you to see it.'

Roz

I'd gone from looking at other people's auras to seeing my own – and bouncing it. It was fascinating. Weirdness on tap. I wondered what it all meant.

'It's really interesting, but what's the point?'

Mia

'Does there have to be a point? Just enjoy it. I do. It's like when a baby touches its hands together for the first time. This is the first time your spiritual hands have touched.'

'Would you agree, Roz, that you are now feeling things you didn't feel before we started working together?'

Roz

'I'm not sure I can come to terms with what it is I'm feeling, but I am feeling something.'

Mia

'The fact you're feeling something is all we want at the moment. You are beginning to awaken your sixth sense. It sounds very grand, doesn't it – your sixth sense?'

'What I find amusing is that if you said to a professional person, "Do you use your sixth sense?", they would laugh at you and say "no". But if you said to that same person, "Do you ever act on gut instinct?", they would probably say "yes". It is part of the same thing. Your sixth sense is …'

I turned to Eric.

'I'm finding it hard to explain the sixth sense simply.'

I got a picture of an old-fashioned radio with a knob that could tune into different channels. With it, I got a picture of a head with bright colours at the eyes and ears as the radio was tuned.

'The sixth sense is like an internal radio tuner. It is a shift in consciousness. You stop seeing, hearing and feeling what you think should be there; instead you tune in to what really is there. You already have this skill. You have just forgotten how to use it. Our job, somehow, is to help you to tune your inner radio to the right frequency.'

Chapter 5

An Impromptu Reading

Roz

That evening, I decided to take Mia out for dinner. As we walked along the city streets, Mia pointed to an old pub.

Mia

'I like the look of that, let's go in there.'

Roz

The pub was busy and smoky. We ordered drinks and food, then sat at a small table. Over dinner, I asked Mia what happened when two people's auras touched.

'Do auras mingle?'

Mia

'Even if two people sit very close, one aura will only push against the other, they won't mix. The only time auras mingle is when two people who are in love come together. That's why falling in love feels so good; you experience a closeness to another being of a kind that nothing else can approach.'

'When a mother holds her baby, her aura embraces the baby's aura as if to cover it and keep it safe. But when two people are in love, their auras embrace each other equally. The magical feeling of intimacy and closeness is because of the aura connection.'

'Emotional disharmony stops the auras mingling. Disagreements subconsciously bring up a barrier so the auras can't interact in the same way. That's why it hurts so much in a love relationship when things go wrong – and that's why some people become rainbow-chasers, moving from relationship to relationship looking for the initial high that comes when the auras mingle.'

Eric came in then and I told Roz what he said: 'Eric says, "When your spirit is in the human form it is lonely. To fall in love is to escape that loneliness." Eric is showing me the outline of two people having sex. He says, "When two people are in love and they make love, it is because they are trying to get as close to each other as possible. The closer a being is to another being, the further away the loneliness is."'

I started to think it was a bit sad, love as an escape from loneliness, but then Eric smiled at me and held his hand in front of him, rubbing his fingers together. Tiny little stars came out of his fingers.

'Of course we add a touch of this,' he said.

I shared this image with Roz.

'Eric says you are more than flesh and the stardust touches your spirit. It heightens your senses. You grow through pain, but it can leave cuts and bruises on your soul. The gift of love is the medicine to heal those wounds so you can go on again. Love is what it's all about. If everybody loved everybody else, there wouldn't be one problem on Earth.'

Roz
Over chocolate fudge cake and ice cream, Mia suddenly asked me a question.

Mia
'Can you feel any energies other than the people you can see?'

Roz

I told her I hadn't a clue what she was talking about.

Mia

'I suppose it is a bit soon for that. I chose this pub because of its age. The older a building, the more energy it has stored up. For instance, I know that at the back of this building there are deep cellars.'

Roz

'How do you know that?'

Mia

'When we walked in here, I scanned out and had a look around.'

Roz

'What do you mean "scanned out"? What were you doing?'

Mia

'I can't explain it, so let me ask Eric what I do.'

'Eric,' I called.

I saw fog in my mind and, as it cleared, I saw his face. He said hello to me and then he said, 'Good evening, Roz.' I passed on the greeting.

Eric told me, 'That chair you're sitting in isn't doing you much good. There's not enough support for your back. And uncross your legs because that's not helping you either. Why be uncomfortable when you don't have to be?'

When he first comes in, Eric often makes a practical, down-to-earth comment about the physical situation I am in. I don't always take his advice but this time it was easy, so I changed chairs and immediately noticed the difference. I resolved – once again – to listen more to his advice.

Then I asked him, 'How can I explain what I do when I'm scanning out?'

He showed me a picture of myself sitting in a room, surrounded by my aura. Then the aura expanded and kept expanding until it went through the walls of the room and filled the whole house. When it reached the house's limits, my aura shrank back to its normal size around me.

I told Roz what I was seeing.

'When I scan out, I feel the building or the area, checking out the atmosphere. Then I get flash images of parts of the building I haven't yet physically seen.'

Roz

'So if I asked you what was on the floor of my bedroom, could you tell me?'

Mia

'Sometimes I can describe a room I haven't physically seen, but it doesn't come to order. When I scan out, it's the same as when I start a reading. I don't care what I see. I'm not looking for anything in particular.'

'I picked up the cellar in the pub because it has a strong spirit presence. It came to me very quickly. As soon as I got the picture of the cellar, I had the image of a slim woman who was alive over a hundred years ago.'

Roz

'So you think this pub is haunted?'

Mia

'More like visited. A haunting is where a spirit is stuck in a place. A visit is just a visit from a spirit to a place that it knew well. A haunting feels sad because the spirit is stuck, but the energy here is quite light.'

Roz

I tried to sense some of the things that Mia had picked up, but it just felt like a busy pub to me. As the waitress came to clear the plates, Mia started talking to her.

Mia

'Is there a cellar at the back of this pub?'

Roz

The waitress confirmed that there was a large deep cellar at the back of the building.

Mia

'Being an old pub, are there any ghost stories connected to it?'

Roz

'It's funny you should say that,' the waitress replied. 'The other evening, I'd turned everything off and pulled the plugs out and, just as I was about to leave, the jukebox came on. It was plugged back in. And a record had been selected and was playing.'

'The landlady has got a daughter, she's five, and the other day she told her mum she keeps seeing a lady walking around in the pub. But the landlady can't see anything.'

It was eerie. Mia had not told the woman what she had seen and yet the woman had confirmed everything.

'So, are you into all that kind of thing, then?' the woman asked Mia, interested.

Mia

'Yes, I work as a psychic, and the reason we came in here tonight was because this pub looked really old.'

Roz

The woman suddenly became excited.
  'Do you do readings for people?'

Mia

'Yes, amongst other things.'

Roz

The woman sat at our table and thrust her palm out towards Mia.
  'Can you tell me anything?'

Mia

'I don't work like that.'

Roz

The woman asked, 'How do you work?'

Mia

'I work with eyes and auras.'

Roz

The woman said, 'I'd love to have a reading with you.'

Mia

'I'm absolutely inundated with people wanting readings and I haven't got space until the end of next year.'

Roz

Undeterred, the woman asked, 'Can't you tell me anything now?'

Mia

'I normally sit in a quiet room with a tape machine and do it properly – it's not a game. And sitting in a pub after having a few drinks isn't really a spiritual situation.'

As I looked into the woman's eyes, I could see her disappointment. It's all very well having rules, but I was starting to sound a bit pompous. I thought to myself: what the hell – it can't hurt.

I connected with her aura and eyes, emptied my mind and waited to see what popped in. I wasn't using any specific visualization techniques, as I did with a formal reading, but I knew that whatever was important would show itself.

Roz

One minute Mia was saying, 'No, I can't do it', the next she was talking about decorating, suitcases, an empty room, contact from Australia and the fact the woman was worrying about her relationship with her husband. The woman said nothing during the reading so I had no clues as to Mia's accuracy.

As Mia finished, the woman said, 'Oh my god, it's so true.'

I listened with amazement as the woman talked about her life and the relevance of the information Mia had picked up.

'The only thing I can't make sense of is the Australian connection,' she said, baffled.

Mia

'Oh you will.'

Roz

After the woman had gone, I said, 'It was fascinating to sit there and be a part of a reading.'

Mia looked embarrassed.

Mia

'It's not really the done thing to give a reading with a drink in your hand. But I was relaxed and she was totally up for it, so it was easy to read. But just because it's easy doesn't mean it's right.'

'None of the information was heavy so no harm was done, but I want you to know I don't make a habit of this sort of thing. To do a good reading, you must be in the right setting. It is not a parlour game or a magic trick. It's real and people's lives are real.'

'I shouldn't have done it. I'm trying to be your teacher and part of that is to stop you making the mistakes that I made. In my early years, I did that kind of reading too often. At the time it's great and interesting, but when I look back, there's always a feeling of missing the bigger picture. The point is not to show off and spin information, you are meant to be helping.'

Roz

I understood all Mia was saying, but I was still intrigued by her detailed accuracy. Moments later, the woman came back to our table.

'I've got to tell you, I've just been talking to my husband.'

We glanced at the bar; a lot of people were now looking our way.

'He went to the solicitors today and he was told he's been left a small inheritance by a friend. I knew about that – what I didn't know was that the friend was Australian.'

Mia gave her a small smile. The woman tried to press her for an appointment for a reading.

'I'd really like to have a proper reading with you, can I go on your waiting list?'

Mia

'You can e-mail me through my website.'

Roz

Mia looked at me.

Mia

'It's time we were going, Roz.'

Roz

We stood up and started putting our coats on. Anxious to leave, Mia went out to start the car while I went to the toilet. On my way out, the woman caught my arm.

'Amazing, isn't she?' she said.

'Yes,' I said. 'I think perhaps she is.'

Chapter 6

Mary and the Bell Tower

Mia

Back at home, on Sheppey, I went over the things I had taught Roz. She knew about people's great need for psychic information. She also had a sense of how to see someone's aura and how to feel her own. What we needed now was for Roz to feel something outside of herself.

When I visited Roz two weeks later, I immediately asked, 'That pub we visited – is that the oldest public building around here? The older a building, the more history has happened between its walls. Buildings can act as tape machines, recording incidences. I want you to see what you can feel.'

Roz

'The George Inn at Norton St Philip is one of the oldest pubs in the country.'

Mia

'That sounds good. Let's go for a beer.'

Roz

Half an hour later, we pulled up at the George. It was lunchtime on a sunny spring day and the car park was full. We walked through the car park to the front of the pub. Suddenly, Mia stopped and pointed to an anonymous-looking concrete area.

Mia

'I can hear the clattering of wheels on cobbled stones. There were once horses and carriages here. It feels like a memory – like something I know. Have you ever been in the situation where you have had a dream and forgotten it, then later in the day, you see something and it triggers a memory of the dream? It's like that.'

Roz

It looked like an ordinary car park to me. I wondered how Mia got the information. Was it floating around in the ether? Was Mia's intuition like an antenna, picking up information long after it had passed?

We walked inside. The inn was a labyrinth of tiny doorways, stone-arched windows and enormous low black beams.

Mia

'I want you to see if you like the building and its rooms. I don't mean the decoration, I mean the feel of the place.'

Roz

Inside one of the low-ceilinged bars, we ordered some drinks. The floors were covered by wide wooden boards. The walls were made of great chunks of stone. There was a log fire in a grate so large that a man could have lain in it.

We took our drinks into a smaller bar at the back, which was empty of people. As I took my jacket off, I felt something in my body. It was like a vibration, a body tingle.

'Is there something in here?'

Mia

As we walked into the room, I knew it was full of energy but I was surprised Roz felt anything so quickly. My mind was being bombarded by images but I didn't want to feed Roz information.

'There's loads of stuff in here. But it doesn't mean ghosts, Roz. It can be the situations and emotions that have been lived in this room. What can you feel?'

Roz

'I can't describe it. A gentle buzzing in my body. It's a bit like the sensation I got when I bounced my aura between my hands, but it's all over my body.'

Mia

Images and words were coming at me but I didn't want to influence Roz, so I fished a piece of paper out of my bag and started scribbling.

Roz

'The buzzing has stopped and I can't see or feel anything now.'

Mia

'Don't worry about it, let's walk around the building.'

Roz

Small corridors led into other bar areas. In each room, Mia asked if I could feel anything, but I couldn't. Outside in the ancient cobbled courtyard, we sat on a bench opposite a balcony that had a sign above it saying 'Residents Only'. Mia seemed lost in thought and I suddenly really wanted to walk along the balcony, so I ignored the sign and climbed the steps.

At the end of the balcony, I stopped and looked down over the beamed edge. Mia was looking at me, smiling.

'It's buzzy here too, Mia, I think. I don't know what I'm saying really, but I feel tingly.'

Then all of a sudden, it was as if the spell was being broken. What was I doing? I wasn't even meant to be up there. I felt silly. I was getting carried away with the whole thing, making things up.

Mia said nothing as I went back down to join her. As we left, we asked if there was any information about the pub. The woman behind the bar gave me a sheet of paper entitled *The Brief History of The George Inn*. I tucked it into my pocket and we walked back to the car.

In the car park, sitting in the car, Mia asked me what I thought of my experiences in the pub.

'I thought perhaps I felt things, but I'm pretty sure now it was my imagination.'

Mia

'It's good that you are questioning what you felt, but let's take it slowly. When we took our drinks into that quiet bar and you felt something there that interested you – that's the first time it happened. But when we went to the other rooms you didn't get anything else, even though you'd already experienced something – so you would have been far more open to feeling something.'

'Then, when we went into the courtyard, what made you go up those steps?'

Roz

'I just wanted to.'

Mia

'There was a sign saying "Residents Only", but you had a feeling you wanted to go up there. The strongest energies I felt were in those two places. I didn't tell you something was there, you felt it. If you were imagining it, how come you felt it in exactly the same places as I did, and nowhere else?'

'Let's just stick to the facts for the moment. You felt something in the first place and the last place and nowhere in between.'

As I looked at Roz, I remembered the early years when I was seeing and hearing things but desperate for logical explanations. It took me years to come to terms with the fact that what I was feeling was real – and here I was expecting Roz to accept it all in the space of a few weeks.

I decided not to argue the point. I wanted Roz to come to terms with things at her own pace, so I changed the subject.

'I didn't want to influence what you felt, but while we were in the pub I made a few notes. Let me show you what I've written down.'

It was getting cold in the car, so I turned the heating on and pulled the piece of paper out of my bag.

'In the first room – the one you had the feeling in – do you remember the large painting on the wall of the lady in the blue dress with the wide lace collar?'

Roz

'I think so. The picture looked as if it was from the eighteenth century.'

Mia

'As I looked at that picture, I got the name Mary. Then I heard a female voice. It was like listening to a faint sound on a radio, fading in and out of range. The words "Mary Mary" kept echoing around me, then "the courthouse … bell tower", then words I couldn't make out.'

'Suddenly I had a picture of a noose. The familiar noises of the twenty-first century faded and I was surrounded by the wooden floors and rough stone walls that would have been familiar to Mary hundreds of years ago. I was hearing the same sounds she

81

would have heard – soldiers drilling, shouts, commands and ban-
ter, snatches of conversation and laughter, the clanging of swords.
It was as if somebody knew my curiosity about the building and
was telling me things about it.'

Roz
'So, are you telling me that what I felt was a ghost?'

Mia
'It could have been a ghost – I was certainly hearing one – or it
could have been the energy left over in the room from all the lives
that have been lived there. The air in the room was full of
emotions, which had become an energy. Just as you could feel the
bounce of your aura between your hands, so you were feeling the
pressure of the emotions within the walls.'

Roz
I wasn't sure what I believed. I took *The Brief History Of The
George Inn* out of my pocket.

'You were right about the horses, it says that by the latter part
of the seventeenth century, The George had stabling for ninety
horses.'

The leaflet also said that the pub had received two famous
visitors, Samuel Pepys and the Duke of Monmouth. The courthouse was mentioned, as was the hangman's rope.

I read aloud to Mia, 'At Norton St Philip 12 men were hanged
at the crossroads by the infamous Judge Jeffries who is reputed to
have held court here.'

Mia
'That makes sense then.'

Roz

It had been a pub for over 700 years and yet Mia had picked up information about a court and hangings. She was nonplussed at her accuracy but I was amazed. I carried on reading.

'And the battle – the swords and soldiers. It sayst "Monmouth, an illegitimate son of Charles II, used the building as his headquarters after his retreat from Bath on 26th June 1685. The rebel army was defeated at the battle of Sedgemoor on the 6th July."'

Mia

'That explains the soldiers. But I'm not finished yet. I want to go and find Mary.'

Roz

'Are we going back into the pub?'

Mia

'No, the voice said something about a bell tower, so I want to check out that church we drove past at the bottom of the hill. You know you had a feeling to go up the steps in the pub, well I have the same sort of feeling to go to the church. I don't know what we're looking for yet, but I feel the need to find Mary.'

As we drove off, I pondered the fact that people imagine psychics get all their information clearly. In my experience, it's not really like that. Often, when you get caught up in a psychic investigation, you get bits of information, then you have to use practical detective skills to put it all together.

Sometimes you don't know what you're looking for until you find it, but usually it is about righting a wrong or clearing the reputation of a person who is dead. Strong feelings of injustice can keep spirits earth bound.

Once I had a haunting at a fairground in Margate. Legend had it that the ghost was a young prostitute who had been murdered. When I got to talk to her, she told me she was not a prostitute and wanted me to clear her name, which I did.

Roz

At the bottom of the hill, we parked the car and got out. A sign told us that we were about to enter the Church of St Philip and St James. We stood outside for a while and looked up at the tower, it must have been about 70 feet high.

The church was situated in the middle of a graveyard and, as we walked towards it, Mia stopped to peer at the names on the gravestones. Old and worn away, the lettering was hard to decipher, but Mia was undeterred. She stopped and looked at every stone.

Mia

'I'm looking for Mary.'

Roz

Mia was enthusiastic and full of energy. It was as if she was on a treasure hunt, but I felt spooked. We didn't even know if Mary existed and Mia was looking for her grave – looking for a dead person. I tried to be professional and peered at the gravestones with her.

We found three gravestones with the name Mary on them, but Mia dismissed them. They didn't appear to be what she was looking for. We reached the front of the church and stood by its gates.

Mia

'I don't understand, I've got bell tower in my head and the name Mary and I know this is the church, so why didn't I feel that any of those graves were right?'

Roz

'Maybe we need to go inside the church and find the bell tower.'

Mia

As soon as Roz said it, I knew that was where we needed to go. Even though I'd done this sort of investigation many times before, I'd missed the biggest clue. It was so obvious, I could have kicked myself.

Roz

The church door was open. Inside, it was empty and the still, dust-filled light made me feel like a trespasser. Mia and I started to talk in whispers. We walked to the other end of the church and found a small chamber. There was a large, stone plaque. It said that the bell tower had been erected by 'the disconsolate widow' Mary Ponting.

It also said that the church housed the remains of her husband Theophilus and her two children, a son who died an infant and a daughter who died at the age of 10. Right at the end, it said that Mary herself was buried in the church in 1805, aged 73.

Mia

So often these investigations end with me having to send a spirit over, but Mary simply wanted to let me know who she was. At this point, I also realized she was not a stuck spirit. She was just visiting, just saying hello – as spirits do now and again in order to come to terms with their life on Earth and to reinforce the emotions and feelings they experienced during that time.

I knew that I had found what I was looking for because the pull to try and find Mary had stopped. There was no urge to keep looking.

'It's alright Roz, it's finished. I've found her. We can go now.'

Roz

In the church porch, I stopped in my tracks.

'What's that noise?'

I looked up at the old oak rafters. It sounded as if a large animal was up there, breathing very loudly. But there was no break in the sound, it was one continuous breath. I'd never heard anything like it before. What could it possibly be? There must be a frightened animal trapped up there, but what kind of animal would make that noise?

Mia was looking calm, head cocked to one side, studying the sound.

'What on Earth is that?'

Mia

It was Mary saying goodbye, but I didn't want to put that in Roz's head.

'I often hear strange noises, Roz. Don't worry about it.'

Roz

I was standing in a church that was ancient and deathly-silent and there was a strange loud breathing noise above my head. I didn't like the fact that I couldn't find an explanation for it. Suddenly Mia spoke to the rafters.

Mia

'Can you make it any louder?'

Roz

And, with that, the noise stopped.

Chapter 7

Protection

Roz

As soon as we got back to the cottage, I started making a fire. I was scared and wanted to keep busy. But no matter how much I chopped kindling and ripped newspaper, I couldn't stop feeling panicky. My reality was shifting. Everything was being turned upside down.

That noise in the church had really freaked me. This wasn't gentle predictions about my future or pleasant aura-bouncing. It was one thing to have a warm, glowing spiritual feeling – but quite another to hear loud breathing in an empty church. Why hadn't Mia warned me that we were entering horror movie territory? I felt distrustful. Without her, none of this would be happening. What was worse, she didn't share my panic. She thought this was all totally normal.

Mia

I didn't need to be psychic to read Roz's hostility. Her silence made it all too obvious. Standing in her kitchen, making coffee, I called on Eric.

'Do you think I've pushed Roz too far, too quickly?'

'No,' he said, 'it's going to be alright. How can she work in our world if she doesn't know it exists? How can you explain wind unless you've felt it on your face? How can you teach a potter to make a pot without the clay to work with?'

'Anyone would be unsettled by these experiences, but it's also interesting how quickly they can come to terms with them. People will either denounce their experience or accept it, but it is never left as grey.'

'Don't let Roz hide from the experience, but don't tell her what to believe or how she should interpret what she sees or feels. She must come to her conclusions by herself.'

Again, Eric's words made total sense to me. I could not force my beliefs down Roz's throat. She had to decide, on her own, if she was ready to accept this new information. I took longer than I needed to make the drinks. I was trying to form the right words. The most important thing was to ease her fear.

In the living room, Roz was sitting on large cushions in front of the fire. I handed her a mug and sat on the sofa.

'Are you alright?'

Roz

'I don't know. I'm not sure what I think at the moment.'

Mia

'That's understandable. You've had a lot of experiences in a short time.'

Roz

'Six week ago, I couldn't even see an aura. Now I've seen auras, I've touched auras – I've even played with my aura. I've been dragged by feelings to go up stairs I shouldn't climb. Now I'm hearing noises that can't be explained. Are you messing with my head?'

Mia

'I understand if you feel mistrustful. Up until today, you felt safe and comfortable with me and now it's as if I've become the enemy. But there's a reason for everything I've done.'

Roz

'Why did I hear that noise? I've never heard anything like that before.'

Mia

'We've been making you aware of your aura and this has energized it. By doing this, we have started the awakening of your sixth sense, which will amplify your other senses. In other words, you are becoming aware that there is more out there than your ordinary senses pick up.'

'When you don't want to be sensitive, you don't have to be. I've shown you how to see, feel and hear things, but it's even easier to show you how not to. Nobody has to be psychic. You can block it.'

Roz looked up and made eye contact with me for the first time since we left the church.

'The reason for these experiences isn't to scare you; it's to show you the world I think you can work in. This is the awakening and it will have a snowball effect. Each little bit you experience will make it easier for you to experience the next little bit. But we can press the pause button, if that's what you want.'

Roz

'Is that true? Can I stop all this?'

Mia

'If you're worried you can learn to shut down. I know it might be hard for you to believe, but I once felt the way you do now. When

Eric first started talking to me, I was terrified. It took me months to find somebody who could help me. She was a healer at a spiritualist church and she taught me a technique for shutting down.'

'The technique wasn't just for me. It can be used by anybody who has opened up their sixth sense and is starting to lose their nerve. It's as simple as this. Sigh and drop. Then imagine your aura all around the edges of your body. Hold onto that image in your mind and picture a rain of gold above your head. It rains until your aura is completely coated in gold.'

'Gold is the colour of goodness, spirituality and strength – it is the highest colour. With this visualization technique, your sixth sense is sealed back in you and your aura stops being sensitive to the atmosphere around you.'

Roz

'Using my imagination is going to stop me being scared?'

Mia

'I know it sounds strange, but that little visualization is all you have to do. In the beginning, when I needed to close down, I was surprised how easy it was to do – and how effective. It doesn't matter right now if you believe in it or not, just do it.'

Roz

I sighed and dropped and closed my eyes. I imagined the rain of gold clinging to my aura and, strangely, I began to feel soothed.

'I've done it, but it takes a lot of effort to keep the gold image in my head. What happens if the image disappears – do I lose my protection?'

Mia

'Once you've imagined yourself cased in gold, it doesn't matter if the picture goes. In fact, you can forget all about it. It's done.'

'Now open your eyes and think of something really practical and basic that you need to do – like cooking the dinner or doing the washing. The key here is to take up the reigns of your physical life. The basics of life are always the most grounding.'

'Any time you want to, you can use this technique. Believe you are shut down, and you are. The visualization aids your belief and the practical physical chores ensure your groundedness.'

Roz
'Do you go through this process when you're working?'

Mia
'No, it's back to that word "belief" again. The imagery technique is useful in the beginning. But later, as you know that you can switch on and off, you only have to think it and do it. That's my shortcut.'

* * *

Roz
Later that evening, chopping vegetables for a curry, I had an enormous sense of relief. I had a get-out clause. There was a key to leaving this scary place and, knowing that, gave me some control. It was no longer quite so frightening.

* * *

Roz
It was Saturday morning. Lying in bed with my boyfriend Mark, I told him about the noise in the church. He was intrigued and started coming up with a list of questions for Eric about guides and the afterlife. I went downstairs to make us some coffee.

A few minutes later, I heard Mark calling me. He was sitting up in bed, looking excited.

'You'll never believe this,' he said. 'After you left the room I decided to try an experiment. I was lying here thinking: "If my watcher is about, give me a sign." I repeated it in my head a few times and, while I did, I was staring at the mirror and really concentrating. Suddenly I saw the mirror move.'

It's a small face mirror in a wooden frame. You can position it on its wooden pivot but, once rested on its axis, it is actually quite stiff and hard to move. It couldn't have moved by itself.

'It was a significant amount of movement,' Mark said. 'It moved about an inch.'

I was amazed that Mark had tried to make contact with the supernatural, and even more taken aback that he'd succeeded. It was tangible magic and I wished I'd been there to witness it. Unlike the noise in the church, it didn't scare me – perhaps because it was happening to Mark and not me.

When I went out of the room to finish making the coffee, Mark tried asking his guide to move the mirror again, but nothing happened.

'We've got a day to ourselves,' he said when I came back. 'Why don't we go to the church and see if we can hear anything?'

That afternoon, we walked through the graveyard. Mark was calling, 'Mary, where are you?' We split up and searched the graveyard for Mary Ponting. The last grave Mark came to, at the far side of the church, had her name on it. He called me over.

'It's nice to know it's here,' I said.

We'd found what we were looking for. We went into the church. The cleaner was there, dusting. No noise. No spooky atmosphere. Mark said it was a bit of an anti-climax, but I was relieved. Sharing it with Mark made the whole thing feel a lot more normal.

Chapter 8

Visualization

Mia

I felt relieved to be going to see Roz. Behind me, I'd left a chaotic house with a plumber trying to fix a leak, a daughter mopping up a flood and a cat with a serious litter-tray problem.

It was a long drive to Bath and I spent the hours wondering how Roz had got on in the time we'd been apart. I hoped she was feeling less scared and had grown more comfortable with the experiences we'd had. I was very aware that I'd distressed her. I tried to think of lighter lessons that she might find enjoyable. I started talking to Eric.

'Eric, have you got any ideas where I can go next with this?'

'Let it evolve naturally,' he replied.

'I'm meant to be a teacher here, Eric. I'd like to turn up with at least one lesson, one idea.'

'This journey is for you as much as it is for Roz. Let it evolve.'

Getting straight answers out of Eric was always worth a try, but I must admit I hadn't expected much more than I got.

Over tea and toast with marmalade (a late morning ritual I was beginning to associate with Roz), I listened to her and Mark's adventures. I felt quietly pleased. Not only was Roz less scared, but Mark was on a journey too.

After our paranormal experiences, however, I knew we needed

something more grounded. Back to basics. It was time to start working with visualization.

'Do you have a question you'd like an answer to? It will be easier to work with the question if it requires a simple yes or no answer.'

Roz

'I've just had a row with a neighbour. Should I leave it or try to speak to her?'

Mia

'Good – nice and basic. I want you to sigh and drop. Now close your eyes. Visualize two telephones in your mind; one is in your hand, the other stands alone. Think of them as two different pictures side by side.'

Roz

'I'm not sure I'm a very visual person. I can't really see anything.'

Mia

'If it's hard to imagine pictures, the simplest thing is to visualize two dots of light, one red and one green. Red is no, green is yes. Go through the same preparation and see which colour becomes bigger or brighter. That will be your answer.'

Roz

'That's not really working either.'

Mia

'That's okay. Let's try something else. You're a literary person, try words. Visualize the words "yes" and "no" in a line, next to each other but with a gap between. Can you do that?'

Roz

'The word "no" is pulsing towards me.'

Mia

'To make sure this is the right answer and not an emotional one, you must forget the question and all the emotions that go with it. Make sure that in your image of these two words, they start in the same position and strength as each other.'

'Try to think that it doesn't matter what the answer is. When you are as relaxed and in that space as much as possible, see which word changes and that is your answer.'

Roz

'It's very quick. The word "no" has got bigger.'

Mia

'That's your answer.'

Roz

It was wise advice. If I'd rung in the heat of the moment, it would have stirred things up again. It was better to let things settle. In fact, not calling was my preferred choice – my first instinct.

'I think I had a gut instinct about not calling.'

Mia

'Gut instinct is a source of spontaneous information. It is the first step of awareness. When you think of somebody that you haven't seen for a while and feel a need to see them or speak to them and then find out they've been unwell, that's gut instinct.'

'It's when the phone rings and you know who it's going to be. It's seeing two people having a conversation and knowing what one of them is going to say. Gut instinct is when you're not trying, you "just know" something. It is the last psychic ability that is acceptable in our civilized world and it is innate in all of us.'

Roz
'Can we enhance it?'

Mia
'The way to enhance this natural skill is never to try for it and to learn to trust it.'

Roz
'But how do I know the difference between gut instinct and my imagination?'

Mia
'Intuition is a quiet voice and you have to be calm and still to hear it. By contrast, imagination has a loud voice filled with vivid pictures which excite the emotions. Imagination has a question mark with it. Gut instinct is a quiet sense of knowing, it just is.'

Roz
'Can I use it to help me in my day-to-day life?'

Mia
'You can harness it to help you make choices, as we did just now. It is like learning to play an instrument. The more you practise, the better you become. If I have an important decision to make – there are two paths and I can only take one – I first sigh and drop to relax.'

'Then I let the emotion about the paths fade and let my heart feel which one is right. The further you get away from the emotion, the easier it is to feel the pull of the true path. Letting go of the emotion is the key thing.'

'Everything changes constantly. When you realize that everyone's emotions are shifting from moment to moment it helps you understand the intricacies of human nature. It helps you to not obsess with how you are feeling at the present moment but to give time to watch your emotions change. It stops knee-jerk reactions.'

'The thing is to stop resisting whatever you are feeling, roll with it and know – deeply know – that whatever you are feeling, it is going to change. It helps you not to take yourself – and any situation – so seriously.'

'This understanding can help through the deepest grief as well as in minor rows like you've just had. Ride the wave rather than let it crash down on you. Being psychic isn't just about predictions and spirits, it is also an awareness – being able to step out of yourself and look at things in a more objective way. The human thing to do is to put our own feelings first, but the spiritual way is to see everyone's feelings as equally important.'

'When someone has had a row, they can't help but feel caught up in their emotions. It's all "I hurt, I need, I want, me, me, me". So much time is wasted feeling hurt when there's no need to. Relationships never run smoothly – that's human nature. Being aware helps you to step back enough not to worry about the minor issues.'

Roz

'That's easier said than done, my emotions come like roller coasters. I don't think "I'm having this feeling" – I am just suddenly in it. How do I stop that?'

Mia

'Visualization. You used it to shut down, and again, just now, to find the answer about the phone call. It can also be used to separate yourself from your emotions – and to look into the lives of others, past, present and future. Visualization builds the bridge between this life and the next; it is a doorway between dimensions. Visualization is the key into the world of the psychic. This is where the magic begins. You're ready to go into the zone.'

Chapter 9

—⁂—

The Zone

Mia

'Many years ago, Eric explained the zone to me. He said, "The zone is a dimension where all knowledge of past, present and future exists. You can call it the daydream place or the space between the last thought and the next. It's a spiritual space and, because of that, when looking at it, you take no emotion with you. It is the plane of knowledge."'

'I've always imagined it as a giant ancient chamber full of rows and rows of old scrolls holding all the knowledge of everything that has ever been and ever will be. Just as a student picks up a text book to get new information, so a psychic visits the zone. It is a paranormal gateway from this world to the next where all dimensions meet.'

'When my sixth sense was so abruptly switched on in my early 20s, I entered the zone without even realizing it and the experiences I had were totally out of control. Eric taught me to tap into the power of the zone and so control my gift. For you the zone will be the doorway to awakening your sixth sense.'

'The idea of the zone is to think of nothing, but that is too hard for most people. We need an image to get us there and the one that works for me is the theatre stage. I picture myself sitting waiting for a show to begin and the curtains are closed. Then, in my mind, I let the curtains open, but there are no lights so it is pitch black. I can see the curtains around the edge and from there I sit back and wait to see what comes.'

'We need to find an image that works for you. It has to have a blank space. You can try visualizing a television screen, or imagine standing in a doorway looking into an empty room. A large cave would work. The idea is to have as little visual detail as possible and maximum empty space. It must be an image you are comfortable with and so can hold for a length of time.'

Roz
'I like the idea of the TV screen.'

Mia
'Make sure you are sitting comfortably. Now I want you to sigh and drop, but take care to do it properly. Remember as you sigh and drop your muscles, really drop them, let them all fall, feel the weight of them. Then breathe normally and forget about your breathing.'

'The next step is to separate yourself from all your emotions. Just for the moment, nothing matters but the screen. And on top of that, you mustn't be interested in the screen. If you get at all excited, interested or worried when the screen comes to life, you will lose the images. Being an impassive observer is the crucial key.'

'If you're concentrating hard enough on the image, your ordinary everyday emotions will take a back seat. The calmer you are, the easier this is. If you're in emotional turmoil, as you were about your neighbour, it will take a lot more work to get the screen up and running, but it is still possible.'

'Remember, just as with all the other exercises, belief is the key. Believe that you are going to see something and it will make it easier for you to get into the zone. If you believe it is possible, you are half way there.'

'Close your eyes. It's best if the room has gentle rather than harsh light so your closed lids aren't fighting against the light. Now bring up the image of the television screen. I want you to concentrate so much on that image that you forget about where you are. The screen is everything.'

'You can help build the image by putting colours around the edges of the screen, buttons and dials if needed. Whatever it takes to help you concentrate your mind on the image.'

Roz
'I can't see anything.'

Mia
'Okay, we're going to use your memory. Visualize your own television and remember what it looks like.'

Roz
'That's better, but it keeps coming and going. I can't hold it.'

Mia
'Sigh and drop and try again.'

Roz
'I've lost it.'

Mia
'Try a blackboard. Visualize a big blackboard.'

Roz
'That's easier. I think because the image is so simple, it's clearer.'

Mia
'Once that image has settled in your mind, look at the centre of

the darkness and, in your mind's eye, rest your vision there. Tell me what you see.'

Roz
'The darkness is moving, it's flickering and wavering. Now I feel like I'm going into it, as if the darkness is around me.'

Mia
'That's fine. You're moving into the zone. Now bring the image of the blackboard back and concentrate on the centre. Watch again and tell me what you see.'

Roz
'I can't see anything, just black ripples. Now I am getting something. I can see the hazy image of a child's bucket and spade, but I'm not sure I'm really seeing it. I'm sensing it. The outline is not clear, but I know what it is.'

Mia
'When you're starting, if you can believe that the image you see is psychic, rather than something you have put in your mind, then the image becomes clearer and easier to see. So see the image, acknowledge it, but let it go, don't hold onto it.'

Roz
'The sand underneath the bucket and spade is wet.'

Mia
'Let the image go. Go back to the blackness of the blackboard.'

Roz
'I can see the outline of an adult holding a child's hand. I can't see any features or detail, just the outline like a silhouette.'

Mia

'Just look. Don't get interested. Are the adult and child by the bucket and spade on the sand?'

Roz

As Mia asked the question, I realized there was more information in the image.

'The bucket and spade are close to me and the people are much further away. The child is holding a teddy bear. It's a lovely image, the child feels safe.'

Mia

'It doesn't matter what you see, you're just looking. Emotions block clairvoyance, try to be an impassive observer.'

Roz

'I've got different images coming quite quickly now. A silver coin under water, a brown shell, an orange fish. The fish is moving a lot and I think it's got more colour than anything else I've seen. It is orange and very ripply.'

Mia

'Let it go. Go back to the black space.'

Roz

'I can see a wide mouth of teeth.'

Mia

'Is it scary?'

Roz

'No, it's smiling and now it is becoming a clown's face with a red nose and white painted eyes. Now it's triggering a memory of a toy clown I had when I was a teenager. I can't see anything else. My mind is going blank.'

Mia

'That was really very good for a first attempt. How do you feel?'

Roz

'Relaxed and floaty.'

Mia

'Nice feeling, isn't it? When most people do this for the first time they will be lucky to get a couple of flashes of colour or a single image. It can take a few attempts to get started at all. Let's go over what you saw and try to differentiate the true images from the zone and those that came from your imagination and your memory.'

'The bucket and spade were from the zone. We know this because the image was unexpected and unconnected to any thought you had at the time. The sand was probably an extension that your imagination attached to the picture. When you have a bucket and spade, sand is the obvious next thing to see. That's why I asked you to break and try again. The mind has an annoying habit of trying to make sense of things and it takes time to learn the difference between your imagination, memory and psychic surfing.'

'The next picture was of the adult holding the hand of a child who, in turn, was holding a teddy bear. Once again, that was from the zone because it was free of pre-meditated thought. But you couldn't help but add emotion to the picture when you said the child was safe. I brought you back again because, when you look in the zone, no emotions must look with you. Remember to be an impassive observer.'

'Then you went on to see the coin – that was a clear image from the zone. But once you saw it was underwater, you then saw a shell and a fish. Neither of these was from the zone; your imagination broke in and saw images connected with the beach. That's why we started again.'

'Finally, you saw the smiley teeth, which were from the zone. And as the teeth turned into a clown's face, this was still the zone. You were getting quite a solid image but your mind couldn't cope with it, so it dragged an old memory up to try to explain it. We know the first clown's face was from the zone because it wasn't the face of the clown you had when you were a teenager.'

Roz

'This all feels a bit random – what are the images trying to say?'

Mia

'There's no grand point to them. It was just a very gentle way of introducing you to the zone and what it's like to see there. People think that when psychics see they get total detail. But we don't. We get broken images, hazy details, words like whispers on the wind.'

'When you are in the zone you just look, you don't analyze or work it out. The time to make sense of it is afterwards. What I find lovely is that, when people are introduced to the zone, they are nearly always given very gentle images. Images that a child would be comfortable with, like the bucket and spade. It is as if it's deliberately made as comfortable as possible so we look forward to going back.'

Roz

Remembering the noise in the church, I began to feel nervous again.

'Is it dangerous to go into the zone on your own?'

Mia

'Absolutely not. When you go into the zone, your spirit is having a look in a dimension in which it is totally at home. It has nothing to do with other spirits or ghosts or anything scary. You are always totally safe, and if at any time you are uncomfortable, open your eyes, focus on something in the room and you will be back.'

'When I first started going into the zone, I occasionally had scary faces jumping out at me. It was like watching a horror film. I asked Eric why I saw these and he said it was my imagination. So if you ever get this, laugh at it. It is just you trying to scare yourself.'

'You will never stop being bombarded with images that are not psychic. The skill is to recognize the psychic images amongst the rest. It's only through trial and error, time and practice, that the images will start to make sense and give you information that you wouldn't normally be able to know. People don't realize that the key to the information, visions and everything you need as a psychic is not outside of you, it is inside you.'

'The more you do it, Roz, the easier it will become for you to sort out the psychic images from the non-psychic ones. It is also called "opening up" because you are opening your sixth sense. You have just experienced the first stage of psychic sight.'

Roz

'I'm still finding it hard to believe I saw psychically. The whole thing was so close to imagination, so similar to daydreaming. It *was* daydreaming, but I took myself there. That was the difference.'

Mia

'Would you want to do it again?'

Roz

'It was quite relaxing, so yes. I'd be interested to see what happens next time. But that doesn't mean that I believe it's psychic.'

Chapter 10

Guides

Roz

My boiler was playing up and I needed to find the manual. I searched in all the usual places and then proceeded to the unusual ones. I couldn't find it anywhere. Feeling frustrated, I wished Mia had not gone home. If she was here, maybe she'd be able to find it for me psychically.

The manual was in the house and, somewhere in my memory, I had to know exactly where I'd put it. Standing in the middle of the living room, the thought occurred to me that maybe I could find it using Mia's method – the zone.

I sat on the sofa, sighed and dropped. I tried to visualize the blackboard – it required concentration and focusing, and that made me feel less wound-up. I just concentrated on the blackness.

I visualized the manual – a black and white brochure with the name and make of my boiler on the front. Then, in my mind, I went to each room in the cottage. I noticed that I kept coming back to my study. I thought: I bet it's in there. And that feeling grew stronger.

Then, on the blackboard, I saw that the manual was lying on its side and there was something blue on top of it. I had a feeling that it was underneath something. I decided to have a look and see.

I went into the study and looked at my bookcases, which I'd scoured over and over, but this time I was looking for something blue. I noticed a blue plastic folder with its spine towards me. I pulled it out, opened it up and there inside was the manual.

I was amazed but, at the same time, it made sense. The answer had floated up from my unconscious. Of course I knew where the manual was – what I needed to do was trust my knowledge and give myself a relaxed space to think about it.

I analyzed what had happened. Part of me had wanted to run around frantically searching. I felt driven, and it required a lot of effort to stop and go into the zone. It took faith to do something so whacky, but it had worked.

I realized the benefit this device could have. We can all tap into that space inside ourselves – the ability to think beyond our limits. So much of the brain is unused. Mia was giving me a method – and encouragement – to use another bit of my brain. I couldn't wait to tell her.

'I accessed the zone while you were away,' I told her the next time she visited.

Mia

I was delighted but not surprised.

'The zone is the basis for all psychic phenomena. When I do readings, I do them from the zone. If I go into a haunted place and I want to pick up information, then I go into the zone.'

I knew instinctively where to take Roz next.

'When I talk to Eric, we use the zone. And you will use it too, to speak to your guide.'

Roz

Mia talked about my guide casually as if everyone had one. I'd accepted vaguely that she had one. But me?

'I can't help thinking that what you call guides could be our higher selves.'

Mia

'Your higher self is you, but your guide is a separate being. Some people call guides guardian angels. Some people call them spirit helpers. It doesn't matter what you call them, as long as you believe in them.'

Roz

'So are angels and guides the same thing?'

Mia

'Absolutely. Some people see guides as angels with wings because it makes them less frightening. It's an image they immediately associate with good.'

'Everybody has a guide. A guide is someone who has lived on Earth, but is now staying in the spirit world. The point of existence for every being, whether human or spirit, is to learn and evolve, and being a guide enables them to carry on learning. Everybody who dies has a chance to become a guide, but first they have to earn the right – by passing through levels of knowledge and wisdom.'

'Eric says, "Your guide is the friend of your soul."'

'Eric didn't choose me, he got lumbered with me – that's the feeling I've always had.'

'Eric says, "As guides, we don't choose who we will work with, but we know who our person will be before they are born. We join them as they are born and stay with them until after they have passed into the afterlife. When the time comes for them to come back to earth, a new guide will then be chosen."'

Roz

'Are all guides male?'

Mia

'In almost all cases our guide is the opposite sex to us.'

'Eric says, "That is the balance that works. And the guide, for their part, learns about the mind and emotions – and the problems – that come with being born of the sex they are not used to. The guide's purpose is to watch, to record, to observe and to help when possible." When you experience that niggling voice in the back of your mind telling you something, that is your guide trying to nudge you in the right direction. It's always up to you whether you're willing to listen.'

'Some people may get help from extra spirits occasionally, but their guide is with them at all times. (Although Eric says if you are in the bathroom or having sex, it is of no interest to them and they fade out.)'

'The main thing to know is that your guide has your best interests at heart. That is an absolute.'

'Your guide is here, Roz. Even though you don't realize it, you've always talked to him – those times, for example, when you are happy or angry and you find yourself talking to the air, saying things like "It's not fair" or "Isn't it great?" Your subconscious knows your guide is there and instinctively communicates with him. So it's not a strange concept or something new; I'm just asking you to talk consciously to him rather than subconsciously.'

'The first thing to know is that your guide will only contact you if you ask him to. When you're ready and you want to say hello, sit quietly, sigh and drop and say hello. It hasn't got to be heavy, there is no special ritual, no spell to cast. Just saying hello is enough. Your guide can read your thoughts – he knows how you're thinking and feeling so he knows that hello is directed at him.'

Roz

I was curious what sort of guide would I have – and how would I know him?

'If I say hello, will I get an answer?'

Mia

'Imagine you're driving in the car, moaning to your guide and then suddenly he starts joining in and talking to you. You would probably crash the car. It's a slow process between you and your guide, to build comfortable communication levels.'

'Your guide knows your breaking point – he doesn't want to frighten you in any way. So even though you may think it would be great to have a conversation with him, the chances are that won't happen for quite a while, if ever. And if at any point you got frightened, he would back off.'

'If you say hello, you may feel air on your cheek or a soft pressure on one shoulder. You may get a whisper of hello back in your mind, but you won't be sure if you imagined it. If you are in the zone, you may get pictures, colours or words. Whatever it is, it will be gentle – so gentle that you won't be sure whether you imagined it or not.'

Roz

'Don't people who are mad hear voices?'

Mia

'When someone is very disturbed, they hear voices which seem to be saying horrible things about them and other people. These are destructive voices. A guide is very different. A guide is gentle and kind and will never impose him or herself or tell you what to do. A guide is more interested in helping you discover who you are.'

'In the beginning, it is best to talk to your guide when you are on your own otherwise self-consciousness might get in the way.

121

But it doesn't matter where you are. That's the great thing about it. As you get more proficient at contacting your guide, he can help you in the most stressful situations.'

'I remember when I was in hospital once, lying on a trolley in a corridor. My husband Andy had punched me and my face was smashed up. I didn't know how bad it was. The accident and emergency unit was frantically busy and I was left on my own. I was so scared. And then I remembered Eric.'

'I closed my eyes and said, "If ever I needed you to help me Eric, I need you now." A wonderful calm enveloped me. It was as if someone had given me a shot of morphine. I went from being a terrified wreck waiting to go into x-ray to telling jokes to the medical staff. Eric took all fear away; no friend on Earth could have done that – and the wonderful sense of serenity stayed with me for the rest of the day.'

'Eric helps me so often in my day-to-day life. I might be worried about my daughter being late home and I ask him if she's okay. It is the feeling he brings which is the most common way he responds. I go from being agitated to being very calm.'

'It works the other way too. I might be worrying about money and I ask him for help and I get more agitated because he says it's going to get worse before it gets better. Then he tells me to stay strong. He is always there and not just for spiritual matters. He is my best friend. He is the one I talk to last thing at night, the one I talk to when things are going great and when they go badly.'

'Your guide won't be able to get you a diamond ring or a Ferrari or give you the lottery results, but he can make you feel better. And that is the most precious thing of all. No matter what you've got or where you are, happiness is the thing you are really looking for.'

'Your guide's main task is to help you emotionally whenever possible. He can't change things, he can only help you deal with them. It is the same with God. If God could intervene and change things on Earth, then we wouldn't have starving or abused children, we wouldn't have war or famine or disease.'

'Our reason for being here is to have experiences for *ourselves*. If God did turn up and deal with every problem we had, we would never learn – just as a child wouldn't learn if its parents didn't let it stand on its own two feet to grow. We are put on Earth to stretch and test our souls and our guides are our emotional battery. They charge us up when we need it. Even when we are not aware of their existence, they try to help us when we are in need. But their help is nowhere near as powerful as when we acknowledge them and ask for their help directly. Then they step closer.'

'It is that magical word belief again. When we accept and believe in our guide's existence, the link between us is strengthened. It is as if there is a piece of string binding us to them and when we acknowledge them, the string of energy becomes thicker, wider and stronger.'

Roz

I wondered about the experience of being a guide.

'Can you ask Eric what it's like for him?'

Mia

'Eric says, "I have certainly learnt patience. We are not celestial beings. We still have our human personality traits, but we are working towards a higher understanding. By helping as a guide, we help ourselves at the same time."'

'Roz, let me explain a bit more. From the moment you are born to the moment you die, the only thing you take with you is the emotional lessons you have learnt – that's what makes the spirit grow.'

'If you meet somebody who has had a basically trouble-free life, they might not have a lot of depth and there may be a selfishness to them that they can't see. When you meet somebody who has been to hell and back, they have a caring depth that has been forged by pain. It is that kind of lesson that continues when you take on guardianship.'

'A guide still has emotions and your experiences affect their emotions. The guide feels as you would feel – the frustration, helplessness, anger, sorrow and the love. Imagine being the guide of a child who is being abused. You love that child as if it was your own and not only can you not stop the abuse, you are forced to watch it. Another human in that situation could at least close their eyes, put their fingers in their ears, deny what is going on, but a guide is a constant witness.'

'If we accept that our emotional experiences on Earth make us grow, then it is easy to understand that our experiences, in turn, help our guides evolve too. But there is always the opposite. Being a guide is not all about pain; your happiness gives them pleasure.'

Roz
'Right now, I'm feeling tired and a bit allergic to my kitten, what's that like for my guide?'

Mia
'Eric says, "Boring."'

Roz
'Are they bored a lot of the time?'

Mia
'Eric says, "The reality is that a lot of your lifetime is pauses between emotional experiences and, as you pause, we rest, but we are never far away. So your itchy nose and tiredness, although irritating for you, has no need of your guide's help."'

'Eric says, "When we are not needed, we discuss with other guides how the job is going – not just what our person has gone through, but what they will go through as well. To keep our personalities intact as individuals we need the stimuli of others, otherwise we could lose ourselves in the personalities of those we care for."'

'Eric is showing me a beautiful picture of a massive park with ornamental fountains, little waterfalls, winding paths, trees, grass, bridges and benches everywhere. Everything is natural. Even the seats are organic, as if they are made from living trees. There are people walking, talking in twos or threes. It feels very serene. This is one of the places Eric goes with other guides.'

Roz

It was a beautiful vision, but it was too beautiful, too comforting.

'Do you expect me to believe that?'

Mia

'Of course I don't expect you to believe it straight away. I've just told you what I know and, hopefully, you can find out for your-self when you begin to communicate with your guide. So shall we try? Remember, it's not a big deal, it's just as if there is some-body in the room you are saying hello to.'

'Relax, sigh and drop, empty your mind. Close your eyes. Whatever visual image you need – empty stage, TV screen, black-board – try to see it now. The visual imagery is just an aid to help you find the blank space.'

'Now, don't expect anything. Remember, the same rules apply here: try not to have any emotional connection with the space – you're just observing. Then say hello in your mind and say it as if you are calling into the darkness.'

'With that simple word, you acknowledge the presence of your guide. That is a massive, important beginning. You are saying, "I know you're there and I am waiting for a response. Nothing more is needed."'

Roz

As I said hello, I felt a bit nervous. What if I did get an answer? What if it was real? I waited for one of the acknowledgements Mia spoke about – a disjointed echoing hello – but nothing. After a couple of minutes I opened my eyes.

'I don't think I've got a guide.'

Mia

'He hangs around for decades with you ignoring him and the first time you say hello you expect him to jump to attention. Have patience. Some people take longer than others, but eventually it is possible for everybody to make contact with their guide. Belief is the key.'

Roz

I closed my eyes again. Nothing jumped out at me last time so, this time, I was feeling a little less scared – a little more open. I said hello again and the word hello popped into my head. I dismissed it. It was my imagination of course – my voice echoing back at me.

But I said hello again and this time I saw the world hello typed in white across the black. This was followed instantly by my sceptical thought 'I'm making this up', but I decided to ignore that attitude of mind and try to stay open. I began to let myself follow the pictures that were forming in my mind.

I saw a small coal fire and then one long flame stretched into the sky – tall and thin. Then I saw a low white picket fence with a gate in it. Behind the fence was a garden with flowers like the ones I used to draw as a child.

I began to feel a warmth in my spine and then around my

arms, it was like being inside a small, cosy room. I felt safe, and a bit reluctant to stop my daydream. Eventually, I opened my eyes and told Mia what I'd seen.

Mia

'Let's break it down, Roz, so you can understand better what's happening. The first time you said hello, you felt nervous and had no response whatsoever. That's how it should be.'

'Then you settled yourself and did it again. This time, feeling more comfortable with it, the word hello popped into your mind but you couldn't distinguish between your imagination and a separate voice.'

'So your guide used a format that was comfortable for you – you're a writer so he used print. Then you saw the fire. Now I know how you love your open fire – it makes you feel cosy – so this is an image not many people would have got but your guide knows you'd be comfortable with it. What he did was to distort it with the long flame in a way that your imagination wouldn't.'

'If I told you to imagine a fire, you would see the grate, the fireplace, loads of coals, you might even imagine yourself poking it and feeding it – or your cats in front of it. What you wouldn't imagine, is one single flame going six feet in the air. Also, it isn't in your memory. So he took a cosy picture and put a message in it in the gentlest possible way.'

Roz

It seemed crazy to think that my guide had put those images in my head. Surely I was daydreaming?

'Mia, what you've said is just your interpretation of my daydream, isn't it?'

Mia

'It could have been, but what stands out is that the meanings came immediately without me having to think about them. And I conferred with Eric, and he said I was correct.'

'What's really nice is the gate and the picket fence. The gate was saying the opening is here whenever you want to go through. And any time you want to leave you can. The child's images, like the flowers you used to draw, show you how safe it is.'

'That was wonderful for a first time, Roz. I expected you just to hear the echoing hello or to get one brief image. How do you feel?'

Roz

'I still feel warm down my arms and quite strangely calmed but I can't recollect the images clearly – they've gone.'

Mia

'They always do. If I said to you, "Imagine your cat, Wesley, sitting on his favourite cushion," can you do that?'

Roz

'Yes. I can see that.'

Mia

'If I ask you, in five minutes, to think of the same picture you will have no difficulty at all in recalling it. But images in the zone don't seem to leave an imprint. They come with full force but leave no residue. They are not picked up by the memory.'

'So, what do you think of the zone?'

Roz

'It's one thing to think it's my imagination, quite another to think it's coming from some universal place or person – another dimension. But I like the feeling. And I want to go on.'

Mia

'The fact that you are willing and wanting to do it again, is the best answer you could give me at the moment.'

'For 20 years, I never stopped to think about how I got my information – it was just an automatic deciphering and understanding. By teaching you, I am seeing psychic images in a fresh light. I think it's amazing that guides use simple symbols and gentle words that at first appearance seem childlike. But the more you look into them, the more information they hold. There's information inside information inside information. Welcome to my world.'

Chapter 11

— ❧ —

Dreaming

Roz

A few days after Mia had gone, tired and achy from being at the computer, I put a cushion on the front step and sat in the afternoon sun. Gradually I became aware that I had a warm honey feeling along my spine. It was the same feeling I had had when I called my guide. I decided to go with the warmth and see where it led me. I had a very strong sense of a presence behind me, close, to the left. It was a comforting feeling. Definitely kind.

I was basking in the sensation, when I felt very gently propelled forward until my chin was towards my chest. I could feel the sun on the back of my neck. I was also getting a good stretch on the back of my shoulders. It was very soothing – just what I needed after slouching at the computer.

What was interesting was that I hadn't consciously tried to find a posture that would make me feel better or stretch my spine. It felt more as if that warm presence behind me had somehow manoeuvred me into position. It was like having my own personal yoga teacher.

Was it my guide? At that point, I wanted to believe it was. Since Mia had left, I'd resisted saying hello to my guide again. But now, rather than me trying to contact my guide, perhaps I was being given a bit of help – a practical gesture.

That night I had a strange dream and, unusually for me, I remembered it when I awoke. In the dream, I was told to look at a piece of uncut crystal embedded in a small stone that I had bought years ago. This, the dream told me, would show me how to see colours in auras.

The next night the dream continued. As far I could remember, I had never before had a dream that built on top of another dream. This time, the information about the crystal was more explicit. I woke remembering the words 'the colours will be iridescent'.

I had bought the piece of crystal years ago and, until the dreams, I had forgotten all about it. I had no idea where, in my domestic chaos, the crystal was but I hunted for it for over an hour. I had lots of other things I should have been doing and, as I rifled through drawers and boxes, I wondered why I was going to so much trouble. Unable to find it, I felt a little unhinged. What was all that frantic searching for?

When Mia arrived, I told her about the dreams.

Mia

'The first thing that stands out is that the dream was in two parts. This is very rare. Recurring dreams or nightmares are quite common, but a dream that continues and carries on from the last dream is unusual. It only ever happens if there is a strong spiritual reason for it.'

'I have a recurring dream about going to see my brother Pete. In the dream, he is standing by a gate on a hill. The gate is open but he can't come through it. So I always walk up the hill and go through the gate. When I get there, we have a hug and then walk together until we come upon the same table and chairs.'

'The setting is the same. What is different, each time, is the conversation. It's always relevant to what is happening with the family or me at the time of the dream. Pete knows what is going on and we discuss family issues, particularly to do with his daughter. At the end, he walks me to the gate, we hug again and say, "See you soon." Then I walk down the hill and that's when I wake up.'

'That is a special dream. But I believe most dreams are just our mind's way of filtering the information it has received and making sense of it. Dreams are like a recycling plant where we replay jumbled pictures and emotions so that stuff can be discarded or stored.'

'I think the dreams you had are special – psychic – because they continued from one night to the next. What was also unusual was how the dream continued in real life – when you woke up, you looked for the rock crystal. Your subconscious knew the dream held real and important information. When you woke, you didn't feel stressed – psychic dreams are not scary – they are always calming, upbeat experiences, like Pete and I meeting up.'

Roz
The dreams had been powerful and were still with me. Like Mia, I had been struck by the recurring nature of the dreams – and my frantic morning search for a long-forgotten piece of rock. Perhaps I *had* tapped into another dimension.

'Do you believe you can dream the future?'

Mia
'We all have some dreams of the future, but mostly the memory of them is pushed back into the subconscious and when that event is played out, it stirs memories and we call it déjà vu.'

'Most people would be totally freaked if they started dreaming the future and then remembering it – because you can't change the future. In precognitive dreams you are seeing what will be, not what may be. It is not an easy knowledge to carry.

'People worry that a nightmare where something horrible happens to them or somebody close to them, may be a precognitive dream. But on the rare occasions that we remember dreams of the future, we are always impassive observers of events. And while in the dream, we never experience emotions.'

'In my last precognitive dream, I was standing on a large boat with loads of seats and people. It started smashing into a dock and, even though the twisting, buckling metal was coming towards me at an alarming rate, I was never scared. If it had been a nightmare, I would have been terrified but in the dream I was just trying to decipher what was going on.'

'When I awoke, I knew I'd had a dream of the future but I didn't know where or when it was going to happen. A couple of weeks later, in New York, the Statton Island ferry crashed into the dock, killing many people. When I saw it on the television, the twisted metal of the ship was the exact image that I'd seen in my dream.'

'Nightmares are normally our fears and worries being played in an action sequence. They are not foretelling the future. It doesn't matter how scary the dream, the root is always an emotional worry. You may dream that you are being stalked by a murderer and, in the nightmare, he has killed your friends and is coming for you. The only reality behind this is that, for some reason, you are feeling vulnerable.'

'You could have a dream in which you are suddenly left with ten babies to look after. In the dream, you are thinking no matter how hard I work, I can't possibly keep all these babies safe. Or you might dream that you are trying to hold water in your cupped hands, and the water keeps running through your fingers. These dreams are different, and yet each signifies loss. The emotion under this is that responsibility is weighing heavily on you in your normal life.'

'When you see dreams in this way, it is easier to decipher their meaning and this will take away the fear.'

'Beneath every nightmare, there is always one base emotion – vulnerability, fear, apprehension, grief. It is that simple emotion causing the whole motion picture. Recognize the emotion when you are awake and acknowledge it. Simply acknowledging that the emotion is troubling you decreases its power and, thereby, its activity in your dreams.'

'Even if you can't deal with or change the situation in your daily life, just acknowledging it will put a halt to the nightmare. People spend an awful lot of time thinking about symbols and pictures when what they should really be thinking about is the emotion that was in the dream.'

I was convinced Roz's two dreams were psychic – but there was more to them even than that. I hesitated. I was wary, once again, of blowing her away, but in the end I decided to trust my instinct.

'The words spoken in your dream were kind and informative. Likewise, a guide would never be controlling or authoritarian. A guide is always kind. It's so much easier for guides to talk to you in dreams because there's no resistance. I believe this was your guide's first visit to your dreams.'

Roz

The idea that my guide had come into my dream world seemed very weird, but I was intrigued.

'If he was in my dream, what was he trying to tell me?'

Mia

'Your guide knows more about you than I do. He knows the way you will find it easiest to work. I find it interesting that the crystal he showed you was firstly one that you've had knocking around the house for years and secondly it was uncut and imbedded in rough stone – there's meaning within meaning here.'

'The rock around the crystal represents you now – untrained and unhoned. But the fact that the crystal inside is one you own, shows that you already have the basic tools you need.'

'The word iridescent is an interesting lesson for me. Aura colours aren't solid but, until you told me your dreams, I hadn't realized that I hadn't explained that. They are like coloured lights, they are see-through and they shimmer. He was filling in a big gap that I'd left in the teaching.'

As I spoke, once again I felt moved. I was teaching Roz but I was learning too. I felt amazed that Roz was developing so quickly. As a teacher, I felt I was stumbling through so much of the time, but something was happening. It was natural magic – and I felt we were in good hands.

I had a feeling of wanting to encourage Roz. Eric had been such a source of comfort for me; I wanted to share that with Roz and help her make contact with her guide. I felt she needed reassurance.

'Saying hello to your guide gave him permission to step forward and start communicating. I can't stress it enough but he will only do it at a pace that is comfortable for you.'

'Now you've started opening up and developing, I'd like to give you a tip. It's a good idea to keep a notebook and pen by your bed because the information in dreams fades very quickly once you're up and about. I've no doubt that you received more information in that dream than you've remembered.'

Roz

I made a mental note to record my dreams, but I wanted to stay talking about guides. I had so many questions.

'Mia, are all guides the same age?'

Mia

'A guide is always an older soul than the person they are looking after, but the physical manifestation they choose is the one they are most comfortable with. Eric seems to have survived into old age in the majority of his lives. Most of his understanding and insights probably came when he was old and he is comfortable in that image.'

'I have tried so hard to visualize him younger, but it is impossible. I wanted to see if he had been good-looking as a young man. One of the reasons he gave me for being old when he doesn't have to be, was that it takes all thoughts of good-looking nonsense away and keeps us to the job at hand.'

'When we die, we go back to the age we were at our prime – the age at which we were most comfortable. My nan died at the age of 87. I'd never known her young. One day, in my kitchen, I saw the spirit of a young woman wearing a blue dress with a wide collar and a wide belt around the waist.'

'I saw her smile and swish her skirt from side to side. I felt as if I should know her. Later that day, talking to Mum about it, she recognized who it was and was delighted.'

'"That was my mother's favourite dress when I was growing up," she said.'

'I realized my nan had come back as a young woman to show me how she is, now happy and whole again.'

Roz
As Mia answered my questions, I thought perhaps I was beginning to believe in my guide. That warm honey feeling I associated with him was unlike anything else I had ever experienced. I wanted to know if there was anything I could do to connect more with this feel-good energy, but I didn't fancy loads of exercises or homework. As if reading my mind, Mia spoke.

Mia
'I'm now going to give you a very simple way to access the zone.

You can make use of the time just before you go to sleep to develop your psychic abilities. Most people don't realize that they visit the zone each night, just before falling asleep.'

'When you're drifting off, random images come into your mind and you only remember them if something jolts you awake. This is a good time to practise. In that drifting stage, you let go of all thoughts and your mind is free of direction. It's a good time to try being non-emotional.'

'The same rules apply, you will see things in this drifting zone, but if you try to concentrate on the images, grab them or have an emotional reaction, you'll lose them.'

'When I first became psychic, I had a young family so it was hard to find the time to sit quietly and go into the zone deliberately. I learned to stretch the time of the drifting zone by fighting off sleep. This may not be good advice for an insomniac, but every time sleep tried to overtake me, I would pull back from it and drift some more. It took months of practise to be able to stay in the zone for fifteen or so minutes before I finally fell asleep.'

Roz
'What were the first images you saw when you entered the zone?'

Mia
'For the first couple of months, the only pictures I got in the zone were a few stones and the odd colour. Then, one night, I was in the zone again seeing the same three stones, totally bored with the image but just looking at it anyway, when it stretched into a cobbled street on a hill, and a horse and cart came towards me.'

'It was so crystal clear it took me by such surprise that I couldn't stop the wave of excitement sweeping through my chest and I lost the picture. But when I went back and started again, it very quickly became the full scene.'

'It takes time to see a sequence of events. It starts with random images and you need to practise to get a sequence developing and building, but everyone can do it because we all experience that drifting place.'

'Whenever anyone asks me how they can hone their psychic abilities, I always tell them about riding the zone before sleep. Nobody has ever said that it failed for them – everyone sees something that they haven't put there.'

'The drifting zone is also the best place to contact your guide.'

Roz

'Riding the zone before sleep may be the clearest and easiest place to say hello to your guide, but it is night time and people can easily get spooked just before sleep.'

Mia

'If you're afraid, you can use the blackboard (or TV or stage) visualization techniques we talked about earlier and do them during the day. However, the drifting zone works for most people.'

'Lying in a comfortable position, in the drifting stage, it is easiest to let go of your body. Also, when you are about to sleep, you are not expecting the usual interruptions of the phone ringing or someone needing you for something. These things make it easier to let go and ride the zone.'

'At first, you may only be able to drift for a few minutes before falling asleep. Say hello in your mind and don't expect anything back. You will get a response of some kind. It is most likely to come in the form of pictures, maybe colours. It would be quite unusual to hear a voice or words when you first begin. If you do, it means your guide feels confident that you will be able to cope with it.'

'It was in the drifting zone that I first visited Eric's home. I'd been psychic for about eighteen months – hearing his voice and seeing him a couple of times briefly. One night I was riding the zone when Eric's face appeared clearly and told me to come with him.'

'I could see him walking down a forest path and I tried to follow him in my mind but nothing happened. He was getting further and further away. In my mind I said, "I can't come, I'm losing you."'

'Then he was back near me.'

'He said, "If you are going to come to my place, then you have to bring yourself in first. Visualize that you are standing here with me, but you are not looking at yourself, believe you are here."'

'I closed my eyes. Suddenly I was looking at my feet and I saw them standing on earth and autumn leaves. Slowly I raised my head. All around me was a lush green forest. Shafts of sunlight were falling between trees that were so tall, you could hardly see the tops. A path cut through the dense undergrowth down to a slope where Eric was waiting for me.'

'I followed him into a clearing. There was a fire burning, surrounded by overturned trunks of trees. He told me to sit and then he said, "Feel the tree with your fingers." Even though I knew it was imagination and visualization, I could feel the different textures of the moss and the bark.'

'Then he told me to look at the fire and asked if I could smell it. I could smell the wood smoke. Then he asked me what I could hear. I could hear the fire crackling but I could also hear noises from the forest – the scurrying of animals and movement of trees in the wind. As all my senses came into the scene, it was suddenly so real and he was sitting opposite me on the other side of the fire. I felt a sense of awe to be sitting in a place so magical and yet so real. And all the time it was incredible to think that my body had not left my bed.'

'"Whenever you need to be with me," he said, "come here by bringing each of your senses in with you. I will always be here."'

'I have used the ability to go to Eric's place so many times. Often in the drifting zone just before going to sleep but, with practise, I can now visit at any time, wherever I am. If I feel anxious or need reassuring, I visit Eric's home and I always feel better.'

Chapter 12

David

Roz

I was still feeling unsure about having regular ongoing contact with an etheric stranger. I couldn't imagine feeling what Mia did – that her guide was her best friend. But then she had been talking to him for 20 years.

I was ambivalent but as curious as ever. And I was still looking for that piece of irrefutable proof. Perhaps I needed to see my guide with my own eyes.

The next morning, I asked her.

'Mia, can you help me to see my guide?'

Mia

'There is no point in trying to see your guide unless you're ready for it. If it worries you in any way, your guide will know and won't allow himself to be seen. But you can try it, if you want to.'

'Your most psychic sight is your peripheral vision – the edges of your sight. Most people don't realize that they have probably seen ghosts, spirits, time re-enactments, but they catch them as flickering glimpses at the corner of your eye. It's that sense you have that someone is standing next to you but when you look there is no one there.'

'You may be sitting in a room and you catch a movement out

of the corner of your eye and you think a family member has just walked into the room but when you turn to say hello there is no one there. In the same way, you can see your guide at the edges of your sight.'

Roz

I had the usual mixture of feelings before a lesson with Mia. I was scared that I might actually see something. This thought was closely followed by self-doubt – who was I to imagine I would experience magic?

Mia

'The first thing we need to do is a practical exercise to activate your peripheral vision. Look at me (or an object if you want to do this later) and start to list what you can see directly in front of you.'

Roz

'I can see you and the curtain behind you and the window to your right and the wind chime to your left. I can also see the radiator on your far right. Now I realize I can see much more. The cat basket, the jumbled mess on the floor, your mobile phone, even bits of the bookcase. It is quite amazing, my eyes are naturally seeing all this extra stuff I've not noticed before.'

Mia

'Your eyes are flickering to the sides, stop it. Just stick with what is directly in front of you. Now carry on describing what is around you, to the sides of you, without moving your eyes off me.'

'You can see much more than you bothered to see and this is true at all times. It's easier on the eye if the room is softly lit and – as with seeing auras – the less visual information you have to battle against, the better.'

'It's good to practise at least twice a day, seeing how much you can see by focusing on one spot and not moving your eyes. Then your mind will get used to deciphering that information and expecting it. After a while, you will start to use your peripheral vision all the time. I do, without ever thinking about it.'

'Now go through the sigh and drop routine, but this time keep your eyes open. Just look straight ahead but slightly down. Try to take no notice of what is in front of you, it is of no consequence.'

'The important thing is that your eyes don't move. It is like pressing the pause button on your viewing mechanism. Settle calmly, try to think of nothing, have no expectations – but do have patience. Now, in your mind, say hello. You can say it out loud if you want to. It doesn't make any difference. Your guide is your friend you want to see.'

'It doesn't matter if you blink, but if you do, try to blink slowly. This will keep you calmer. You are trying to create a stillness, so your mind is not busy or caught up in emotion.'

'If you see your guide, he will start as a shadow out of the corner of your eye. If you try to look at him directly, you'll see nothing and have to start again. Keep calm and grounded.'

'Guides always seem to come to the same side of your body. Eric nearly always comes in to the right of me.'

Roz
'I'm not getting anything'.

I tried a few times, but nothing. Absolutely nothing. I felt both disappointed and relieved.

Mia
'You think you may be ready to see your guide, but nobody really knows how they're going to react. I'd been speaking to Eric for months before I saw him. I kept saying, "I want to see you" and he would always reply, "You're not ready". Then one night when

he gave me this same answer, I had a childish tantrum and told him if I was ready to hear voices coming out of the air, then I was totally ready to see him. I also said, "If I can't see you, I don't want to speak to you anymore."'

'I heard the words "So be it" and, in the open doorway, I saw a hovering soft ball of light which expanded to fill the doorway and then, suddenly, a very old man was standing there. He was about five foot six inches tall, the only hair he had left was a few wisps around his ears and the back of his neck. He was wearing an old brown robe which looked as if it was made out of hessian, with rope tied as a belt around the middle. He was leaning on a roughly-made walking stick.'

'His head was slightly to one side and his eyebrows were raised. He had very twinkly blue eyes. It was his expression that registered the most because everything about it teasingly said, "You asked for this, now cope with it."'

'This was what I'd been wanting for months, yet it hit me like a punch in the chest. I was so scared. Then he was gone. I'd accepted I had a guide and was talking to him daily, yet this image of a gentle old man terrified me. He was right. I wasn't ready for it. Your guide knows best and will show himself to you when and if you are ready.'

'Have patience, keep looking on a regular basis and trying to see your guide out of the corner of your eye. But, even if you do start to see him, it will almost certainly be shadowy and fleeting.'

Roz
Suddenly Mia was no longer looking at me. She was looking at something she seemed to see over my left shoulder.

Mia
'It's not usual for me to see other people's guides, but I am seeing the outline of yours.'

Roz

'What does he look like?'

Mia

'He's a tall, thin figure. My feeling is that he's not as old as Eric, but older than you.'

Roz

Listening to Mia, I felt I was under a spell. It was such a beautiful idea.

'Do you know his name?'

Mia

'His name is David.'

Chapter 13

The Sack of Gold

Roz

After Mia had gone, I decided to look for the crystal in the stone again. If there was a message from my guide in that dream, then I wanted to know what it was. I'd been successful when 'psychically looking' for the boiler manual, so why not the crystal?

I sighed and dropped and went into the zone. Once I had the blackboard in my mind, I visualized the crystal and concentrated on it. Again I went from room to room in my mind, but I could not locate it. I had a vague memory of having given it away – that must be why it was no longer in the house.

Waiting for Mia to arrive I contemplated the fact that maybe – just maybe – I had a guide and he was starting to tell me things in my dreams. That was manageable. Not too scary. If I was going to accept that Eric was teaching me, then why not a bit of advice and training from a guide of my own?

The stuff about dreams – I liked all that and had already started to keep a pen and paper by my bed. Just in case. And riding the zone before sleep and experimenting with my peripheral vision, that felt natural, intriguing, exciting even. But what was I meant to do with the rest of the information?

Mia

On my drive to Roz's cottage, I chatted to Eric.

'I'm so pleased Roz has been able to contact her guide. It's easier than I thought. All that worry I had about being able to teach. I think I'm actually enjoying it now.'

Eric said, 'You may be enjoying it, but is Roz? You need to bring some enjoyment back into it for her. Teaching isn't just about giving information, it's keeping the pupil interested and wanting to learn more. So you had better come up with a good idea for today.'

Once again, Eric had stopped me blundering in like an idiot. Chastened, I racked my brains for something to lighten the teaching. I remembered a friend telling me that Bath was near Glastonbury and that if I got a chance, I should go there for a visit. It was Saturday – a good day for an outing – so I greeted Roz at the door with a plan.

'How far is Glastonbury from here?'

Roz

It was a relief to escape another fireside lecture about the machinations of the afterlife. The sun was shining and I was ready for a day trip. We climbed into Mia's car and set off over the Mendip hills.

Mia

I knew that Glastonbury was considered a spiritual place, but I knew nothing of its history.

'Have you been to Glastonbury before, Roz?'

Roz

'It's really beautiful. There is a big hill called Glastonbury Tor with a ruin at the top. I've also been to the music festival, down the road at Pilton.'

Mia

The journey passed quickly, as Roz told me of her experiences performing in the Poetry Tent at the festival. I wanted to take the pressure off, so I said, 'Let's think of this as a day out. If we get a teaching out of it, it's a bonus. The most important thing is to enjoy the day – and climb the hill. It will be good to see the views from up there.'

Miles out of Glastonbury I saw what looked, to me, like a mountain. As I saw it, Roz pointed through the windscreen.

Roz

'Look – there's Glastonbury Tor.'

Mia

My heart sank.

'I was thinking of a stroll up a small hill. Look at the size of that. How long does it take to climb?'

Roz

'About twenty minutes, it is a strenuous uphill climb, but it's worth it. And then we can run all the way down.'

Mia

Roz looked positively radiant at the thought of the climb. I reached for a cigarette, lit it with a trembling hand and, in my mind, shared the moment with Eric: 'I've cheered her up so – do me a favour – keep me breathing till I reach the top.'

Roz

Before we hit the Tor, we browsed the paraphernalia in the town's New-Age shops: cards, crystals, runes, potions, Celtic jewellery, dream catchers, incense burners, joss sticks, weird and wonderful candles and oil burners.

Then we visited the bookshops where there were weighty tomes on everything from self-help to astral projection – auras, spirits, angels, crystals, dreams, psychology, numerology, astrology, past lives, pendulums, fairies.

I was on psychic overload. I bought two packets of incense. Mia tried to find a purse for Tanya, but bought nothing.

Mia

'Okay, time for a cup of tea. Where's a good place to go?'

Roz

'There's a funky café just below the Tor.'

We walked through the door into a kind of grotto, with rivulets of water running over the cobbled stones of the floor. The cave-café was lit by candles and fairy lights. Mia was amazed to find an ashtray.

'What do you think of Glastonbury?'

Mia

'It's very interesting. There's a strong feeling of energy in the whole area, it's been with me since we arrived. There is so much history here. People have been living in this place for thousands of years. I can sense a huge number of lives overlapping, communities stretching far back through time.' I paused, remembering the high street.

'And I've never seen so many New Age shops in one place.'

Roz

'All those shops and you didn't buy anything.'

Mia

'The truth is that I haven't ever needed cards, runes or crystal balls to work psychically. But there's a massive market for all these aids because people think they hold the key to the psychic realm. They search for information and guidance they don't realize they already have.

'I've got nothing against props if they give people confidence and help them to tune into the zone. But what I really believe is that the truth is much more accessible and simple than people think. Everything you need to know is inside you.'

'Let me explain. Before you come to Earth to be born, you are whole, you have total knowledge of your past lives and the afterlife. This is your higher self. When coming back to Earth, all of this knowledge is separated from you and put in a kind of spiritual battery – like a sack of gold – attached to you.'

'When you are on Earth, you have to get through your emotional lessons raw – without the aid of any previous knowledge or the experience of your higher self, but it is all there in that golden sack. There's no need to go looking for information outside yourself. You already know it all.'

'When we die, we go "home", like going home from school at the end of term. It's where we meet up with those we have had relationships with on Earth. We are just spirit in a physical body – our body is like our "school uniform". "Home" is a place where we come to terms with the experiences we've had on Earth and evaluate how we did in this life. Ultimately, "home" is where we really belong.'

Roz
'So what is heaven? And does hell really exist?'

Mia
'I've had many conversations with Eric about the afterlife. Sometimes he answers my questions and sometimes he doesn't. I've only been allowed glimpses and pieces of information, but what I have learned so far is, yes, there is a hell, just as there is a

heaven, but with many levels in between – and all are part of the afterlife.'

'Ultimately, our higher self is aspiring to the highest dimension possible – in other words "heaven". Nobody who walks the Earth is totally good or totally bad. Likewise, no human can go straight to hell or straight to heaven.'

'When you die and go home, you first pass into a waiting area. There your subconscious and higher self are reawakened and reconnected with your conscious self into a complete being. From that state, you look back over your life and judge all the things you have done on Earth.'

I was suddenly aware of Eric's presence beside me. I listened to his voice. He was intervening to provide another piece of the puzzle.

'Eric says it's important to know that at this time of self-judgement you are not alone. Your guide, who has been with you since birth, is also your companion in death. Just as on Earth you might seek the help of a counsellor to come to terms with emotional scars, your guide becomes your ultimate counsellor, someone to talk to and be with, and who helps you to deal with the truth. This is why a person in spirit can't usually be contacted during the first couple of years after their death – because they are going through this process.'

I stirred my tea, aware of the gentle sound of the water running over the stone floor in the café.

Roz
'So "home" isn't the same as heaven, then?'

Mia
'Think of it this way, "home" encompasses those middle dimensions in between heaven and hell, where we are constantly trying to move up to the next level.'

'If a person has done bad things in their life, they can go down a grade in the afterlife, but they would get another chance to come back to Earth.'

Roz
'So obviously you believe in reincarnation.'

Mia
'Yes, reincarnation is what happens to us each time we are sent back down to Earth. As our higher self we choose the experiences we wish to go through in our next life, and often we choose to be born into a certain family or position in life where these experiences are most likely to occur.'

'Remember the sack of gold? It is hidden in your subconscious. This is why you hold memories and images of your past lives in your subconscious, as well as the essence of your soul's personality and whispers from your higher self to guide you in this life. When you have a strong feeling about something or someone, an unexplained compulsion to take a particular action, this is your higher self communicating with you.'

Roz
'Have you ever experienced any of your past lives?'

Mia
'People often undergo past life regression in order to find out who and what they were in previous lives. But I believe that our past lives are not meant to be remembered. I suppose there is no harm in doing it out of curiosity, but it is a waste of energy and there's no value to it either. That is why it is so difficult to achieve successfully. *This* is your life. You have come down to Earth for this experience alone. This life's lessons are the ones being learned and stored, and trying to remember others would be distracting.

On the rare occasions that you are able to tap into past lives, you will only catch fragments of memories and many of these will be quite ordinary.'

'I want to cut through the endless, overcomplicated nonsense that seems to shroud the whole psychic arena and show people how easy it is. The sixth sense is not magical, mystical or unobtainable. It is simply something we are all born with and can develop – without the aid of tools – if we put in the time and effort. And, of course, if we believe.'

'I get so angry when people put psychics on a pedestal – they even try to do it with me and I'm as flawed as they come. Some people seem to think that because I have a psychic ability, I also have saint-like qualities.'

'It's as if people don't believe they have psychic ability so they project their buried skills onto gurus. They are giving away their own power over their lives. I want people to own their birthright. I'd much rather be a teacher than an all-knowing guru. I want to show people what they have inside.'

'And while I'm on my soapbox, I'd like to point out that not everybody who is trying to develop their sixth sense is doing so for the betterment of others. There are a lot of people out there doing it for purely selfish reasons.'

Probably eighty percent of so-called practising psychics are con-artists. One of the most common ways of cheating people is to start a consultation with a very heavy prediction – someone close to you is going to die or become very ill – this blows you away and you lose your concentration for the rest of the reading. It is also very scary. Then they just ramble on for half an hour or more but, because they don't allow the reading to be taped, you have no proof of how rubbish they were.'

'Then there are the ones that tell you you're cursed or have a demon and that it will take many sessions to sort it out – at high expense, of course.'

Mia

The café was now almost deserted. I glanced over at Roz.

Roz

'I don't like the idea of negative influences, possession and the dark side of things.'

Mia

'You're not actively pursuing the darker side and, even if you were, it's unlikely that you'd find anything. And, anyway, your guide will stop all negative interference unless you deliberately call it in. Now I suppose we'd better climb that hill.'

Chapter 14

Avalon

Mia

Forty minutes later, I thought I was going to die. My heart was thudding so hard, it felt as if it would burst. I was gasping like a grounded fish while young children and old people calmly passed me on the hill. As I struggled with the last few steps and reached the top, there was Roz smiling expectantly.

Roz

'Do you pick up anything, psychically?'

Mia

'I feel as far as away from being psychic as it is possible to be. All my attention is taken up with my poor body. Give me ten minutes, Roz. Go and look at the view.'

At last my heart regained its normal rhythm and I became aware of the scene around me. I realized that, even though I was exhausted, I felt alive in a strangely energized way. It was as if the air was full of electricity.

My eyesight felt sharper and the people standing in small groups around the top of the hill, had auras that were shining and moving, brighter than I would normally see them. I didn't need to work at being psychic. As I glanced around me, it was so easy to feel how people were feeling and know what they were doing there. It was like standing on a psychic battery.

I smiled to myself when I saw a young man facing the sun, with a knife held out to the rays. At first sight, a man with a knife on a hill could be worrying, but his aura showed no malice. His colours were ordinary, neither the blacks and reds of dark energy, nor the gold and silver hues of a spiritual power. He obviously thought he was involved in a secret ritual with the sun god, invoking a great divine power, while next to him, a family munched their jam sandwiches oblivious to his would-be spell-casting.

It was much more interesting up there than I'd anticipated. I joined Roz who was standing with her back against the old stone arch of the ruined tower that had been so clearly visible on the way up.

Roz
'It's amazing isn't it? The views are wonderful.'

Mia
I looked down at the stream of people moving up the hill in ant-like procession. What was driving them to embark on such a long, hard climb? There was something magical about this place. I looked at Roz. Her aura was glowing, wider than normal. Every one looked so much more alive on that hill. More vital. I felt healthier than I had for a long time.

'How do you feel?'

Roz
'I love it up here. It always makes me feel good.'

Mia
'See if your aura can feel the air around you, just like you did at The George.'

Roz

'It feels kind of buzzy, like the air is vibrating.'

Mia

'Yes, it does, doesn't it? It's wonderful.'

Roz

'Do you get anything from this ruin, Mia?'

Mia

'My first impression of the building is the word "gateway", but it looks more like a temple or a place of worship. I can clearly see a different building in its place. It was made of wood, with four archways.'

The information board at the top of the Tor gave only partial information. It told us the Tor was steeped in centuries of legend and folklore. Many strange experiences here had given it the reputation for being a place where worlds meet. According to the tourist information, this enigmatic ruin was the remains of a 15th-century tower that was meant to be part of the church of St Michael. But I knew that this was not the first building on the site. Its real meaning and purpose had been lost in the mists of time and all people could do was speculate.

'What strikes me about the scenery is that I feel I already know it, that I've been here before. I don't know if it's because I'm working psychically and being in tune with the area or if it really is somewhere that I have been in a past life.'

I wandered away from Roz and walked around the sides of the ruin. Eric was so easy to communicate with up there.

'So they call this Avalon,' he said.

Avalon – I searched my memory. All I knew about Avalon was that it was the mythical isle said to be the resting place of King Arthur. Legend has it that the dying king was carried away by boat to Avalon, and it is here that he awaits his time to return one day.

'It's as I remember it,' Eric said, 'but it had another name then.' He seemed to be saying this more to himself than to me. I was so surprised that Eric was talking about anything of his previous existence. It had never happened before. The most he let me know about him was when I visited his place in the forest.

I felt that Eric was having a special moment of personal remembrance and I didn't want to intrude by asking questions to satisfy my own curiosity. So I stood beside him in silence.

I'd never been anywhere like this before. After a while I said, 'I didn't know that places like this existed, Eric. It feels like something out of a fairy tale. The energy is strong enough to make you feel you could fly.'

'It has always been strong here,' he said. 'That is why the gateway was built here.'

'Is the gateway the wooden building I saw, or the ruin that's still standing?'

'It was as you saw it. At the right time, the gateway on the crest of the hill is the place where the barrier between this life and the next is at its thinnest. There are many legends – some now lost and not all of them true – but there is a grain of truth behind each one. And even today, with civilization at its most cynical, the power still holds. Feels good, doesn't it?'

Eric was standing beside me looking out over the surrounding hills. There was a strange feeling of companionship with him because, for the first time ever, we stood together looking at something outside of ourselves.

I had the strong impression that Eric was very pleased to be where we were. The look in his eyes showed memories of other times. It was an honour just to be there with him.

I was brought back to the present, by Roz coming to stand beside us.

Roz

'Have you psychically felt anything else?'

Mia

'Just that Eric is so pleased to be here. I'm really glad we came.'

As we started to make our way down the Tor, we saw a group of people talking.

'They think they're witches. Come on, I'll show you.'

Roz

I followed Mia into the middle of a group of people. Most were wearing jeans and jumpers, but one had long purple hair and was wearing a black cape. Mia thrust her hand at her and introduced herself.

Mia

'Hello, my name's Mia. What's your thing?'

Roz

The woman said, 'What do you mean, what's our thing?'

Mia

'What are you doing up here, what are you getting out of it?'

Roz

The woman said, 'We're Wicans and this is a powerful place for us.'

Mia

'I should imagine it is. It's a powerful place altogether.'

Wicca is a broad term for witchcraft. It is an ancient religion based on the power of the earth and being in harmony with nature. It also involves ritual and spell-casting. Do spells actually work? I believe that rituals can reinforce the power of the belief. But that's where the 'magic' lies: in the power of belief. Think of someone recovering from an accident who is told that they will be in a wheelchair for the rest of their life and the power of their belief allows them to walk again. Belief can tap into all of our abilities, even those we don't realize we have.

Wiccans feel that they are able to influence events and people, although most do not believe it is right to directly interfere with another person's freewill. But there are two sides to everything and some people use Wiccan magic for selfish and destructive reasons, for personal gain and power, rather than harnessing the power of nature to help others. I knew that this group of people believed they could work with the dark side.

I wanted to see if the woman with purple hair had the power of her convictions and would admit it to me. The whole time we spoke, I did not break eye contact with her.

'What area of Wicca do you practice?'

Roz
The woman said, 'What do you mean what area?'

Mia
'Good, bad, black, white, negative, positive?'

Roz
The woman said, 'I used to say I was grey.'

Mia
'We both know you can't be grey.'

Roz
The woman said, 'Yes, I know that now.'

Mia

She could not hold eye contact and looked away. She did not have the nerve to say she practised the dark side.

As Roz and I started walking slowly back down the hill, the strongest feeling I had was relief. Thank God they didn't know what they were doing. Playing around, thinking you can tap into the power of negativity, is massively dangerous. There is a dark side and the backlash can be tremendous. Luckily most of the people that play around with the dark side are – just like this group on the hill – too inept to be dangerous.

'The important thing is how you use the power.'

'Eric says, "Once we understand there is a supernatural power we can tap into, then comes the responsibility of how we use it. It is negative to use it for self-gain at the expense of others. It is positive to use it for others, to ease pain and suffering and bring enlightenment."'

'These sound like grand phrases, but we are already making these choices every day in our ordinary lives. Everybody knows, deep within themselves, the difference between good and bad. Being human, we often do things we know we shouldn't – hopefully on a minor scale – but I don't believe that anyone can ever say they didn't know it was wrong.'

'There is a continual shifting of balance between good and bad within each of us and in the external world. What's scary is that, at the moment, bad is winning. There is a sense of despair in the world. News footage of terrible wars, violence, crime, the horrors of disease and famine, all the global catastrophes – as long as these things don't touch our personal lives, we don't care. Most people are so caught up in their own lives and their own problems. We dissociate ourselves from pain and strife and the lives of others.'

'I think in times gone past, we needed each other more. Helping each other was a more normal and instinctive way of life. These days, we view other people's problems as their own. It's easy to think in simplistic terms of a murderer being a bad person and a nun being a good person, but they are just the extremes. All the actions in between – the ordinary mundane ones – count as well.'

'We are all accountable for the choices that we make. But nobody and no action is beyond redemption. Even if you have committed the most heinous crime, if you are truly sorry, your mortification starts to redress the balance. The difference between someone who has strayed down the wrong path, and someone who is truly evil is that evil has no sense of remorse, never feels sorry.'

Out of breath, we stopped to rest on a bench. The sun was still high in the sky.

'I recently had a letter from a man serving a life sentence in prison for murder. He wrote to tell me that he admired my work and hoped that everything I worked towards would happen. Near the end of his letter, he stated that he had chosen the wrong path and done bad things. Even though he'd had a bad upbringing, he said, it did not excuse his actions.'

'As I read the letter, I realized he was saying that he considered me a good person and himself a bad person who had failed and could never make it right. This touched me so deeply that I wrote straight back.'

'I told him: "I want you to know it is always possible to change the balance of good and bad inside ourselves. The fact you admit and know that you did wrong, has already started the change. Think of ways of helping others, even if it's only through writing and talking. Each time you do a kind deed, your soul will become a little bit lighter. It is never too late. It is never finished until the last breath leaves your body."'

Hauling my body off the bench, we continued to pick our way down.

'The emotional lessons we will encounter in our lives are pre-destined. But all through our lives we come to crossroads where we have to make choices, and those choices are ours to make. Whatever path we choose, the emotional lesson will be the same but it will happen in a different situation. This is how freewill and destiny work together. It is not a case of either being in complete control of your destiny or having none at all.'

'Choice is highlighted at a time of crisis. Take the example of a woman in a relationship where she is being battered. The man has the choice whether to hit or not, the woman has the choice whether to stay or not. We know what is right and we know what is wrong.'

'Everybody who walks the earth has an excuse for their behaviour. But, believe me, that won't work when it is time to go home. When you die, every part of your life is replayed and you can't hide from it, you can't delude yourself with excuses as you can on earth. When you are home, there is no such thing as an ego, with all its fears and self-delusions. There is only pure truth.'

'God doesn't judge you; you judge you. We have all experienced that uncomfortable feeling of "I wish I hadn't done that". Imagine how amplified that feeling will be when you have nowhere to hide and you're left with yourself.'

'In child abuse, we often hear that the abuser was abused as a child or they have a drink or drug problem. Amazingly, some even say the child led them on. Whatever their rationalization, their soul will not be able to hide from the truth that it was wrong.'

'It isn't just violence, it can be selfishness, greed, delusions of grandeur – whatever puts you first at the expense of others is wrong. And if you find yourself with any of these notions, take a step back and make a fresh choice.'

'One young man who came to see me had been on heroin for years; he had tried so many times to give it up. He was isolated and in despair. His main question was: "If I kill myself will I go to hell?" In other words, would it be all right to kill himself because he couldn't fight his addiction anymore.'

'It wasn't just the fact that he was on heroin. He had destroyed his parents' lives and they were divorced because of him. He'd stolen from family and friends and had two children that he'd left and hadn't seen for two years. Nothing about his life was of benefit to anyone else.'

'He ended up staying with me for hours that night, drinking many cups of coffee. I told him that this was as low as it gets and if he killed himself, he wouldn't be punished but he'd be sent back to do it all over again. I also told him he was an old spirit and nobody is given a lesson they can't deal with. His future good deeds would far outweigh the bad deeds of his past.'

'I saw him a year or so later. He'd been clean ever since our meeting and was taking a degree in social work. He had access to his children, and his family and friends trusted him again. I was so proud of him.'

'He was determined that he was going to help other young people with drug problems because he'd been there and he'd survived. He felt if he could do it, anyone could. I know when his time comes to go home, he won't be chastised for his earlier deeds, he'll be praised for the battle that was fought and won.'

Near the bottom of the Tor, I stopped again to catch my breath. My legs ached but my mind felt clear and strong.

'When we meet people who seem to have no problems in their lives, it may appear unfair. They make big deals out of little things. But we mustn't judge them, they are young souls and couldn't cope with more.'

'I remember, after my brother died, I was doing a reading for a young woman. The only thing she had in her life to worry about was whether her boyfriend would get back in touch with her after an argument. I got through the reading as quickly as possible and feigned a headache.'

'In the car on the way back, I was ranting at Eric. She didn't know what a problem was. I'd just had my brother murdered, how could I find sympathy for something as trivial as this? That's when I first learnt that what is minor to one person is major to somebody else. Just because she hadn't suffered my pain, didn't mean she didn't suffer. It wasn't her fault that she had never been bereaved. It wasn't my place to sit in judgement.'

'Older souls get harder lessons because they have more strength, depth and experience. Even though they may not remember their past lives, their past experiences do give their soul a strength that it can draw from.'

'We may see it as unfair while we are here on Earth, but being here is not the whole picture. I think the best way to see life is as two ways of going around the world. One is to travel very quickly and remember nothing. That's a young soul's journey. The other way is to keep a journal that you can look back on and remember and never forget. The experiences that really touch your soul are your life's journal; they'll never have to be repeated if knowledge is drawn from them and used.'

Roz

Walking down the Tor I felt exhilarated, both by the place and our conversation. I felt empowered by the thought that we have choice and must take responsibility for our actions. But I also knew that bad things happen to all of us, whatever our choices.

'What's the best way to deal with bad situations?'

Mia

'Firstly, when bad things happen, know that it is not meant against you. It is not a personal thing, no one in spirit is trying to hurt you or abandon you. There's no such thing as fair or unfair on Earth, it just is.'

'Then, change what you can and accept what you can't. Know that nothing stays the same and, no matter how painful, it passes. After it passes, use the knowledge of that pain to help others.

That way no bitterness stains your soul. And remember, the experiences you go through are never in vain, they can only enrich your soul even if they feel painful at the time.'

Roz
At the bottom of the hill, we paused and looked at each other. Mia was smiling broadly.

Mia
'So much for having a day off, eh?'

Chapter 15

—⚬—

Stream of Emotions

Roz

That night I had vivid, wild and chaotic dreams. So many people and things happened in such rapid succession, I couldn't remember any of them clearly but, when I woke, I felt churned-up and exhausted.

When Mia arrived, I was still wrestling with images.

'The last few nights, my mind has been so busy. Do you think the work we're doing is affecting my dreams?'

Mia

'Absolutely. It's a phenomena that happens when people open up. We all have phases where we have weird dreams, but when a person starts developing psychically this is magnified tenfold.'

'When you start to develop your sixth sense, you can't help but disturb locked-away memories. With psychic awareness, comes a re-evaluation of who you are and what's made you that way. You may have the memories when you're awake but, if not, the emotions stored in those memories will rampage through your dreams.'

'It can be a bit unsettling but the intensity won't last. It will eventually burn out. It may be unpleasant, but it is a cleansing. Just as a counsellor encourages people through post-traumatic stress by talking about it and reliving it, so your spiritual self does the same thing. Your subconscious uses weird and wonderful dreams to delve into emotions you won't look at during the day. By doing this it heals.'

'Please don't be daunted and think this is the downside of being psychic. You may wake up feeling emotionally battered by your dreams, but, within an hour, that will settle and your emotions will be steadier and improve day to day.'

'The dreams will go on for quite a while – and they will never stop completely because you have tapped into a new resource. But it is never negative. There is always a good reason for it; there is work being done while you sleep.'

'What you don't have time for or don't want to face during the day will be faced in your subconscious at night. I guarantee there will be mornings when you will wake up with an emotion you haven't felt for years.'

Roz
'Did this ever happen to you, Mia?'

Mia
'When I first opened up, I had a recurring dream of being chased by a man. The man varied but I always woke with a feeling of fear and vulnerability. The dreams related to something traumatic that happened to me when I was 13, growing up on the Isle of Sheppey. I was stalked for months and then raped by an 18-year-old who had become fixated on me. After the event, I never really spoke about it. Years later, when I was discovering my psychic ability, I went through a period of reliving the trauma and I'd often wake feeling emotionally raw. Clearly, I had never fully come to terms with the experience.'

'After a few months, the dreams gradually eased off and I realized the memory no longer held any pain for me. I'd somehow worked through the feelings of terror and vulnerability. I could remember the hurt but it no longer hurt me. I never had to face that rawness again.'

'Dreams help you work through grief – whether you're opening up as a psychic or not. In the weeks after my son Shane died, I could talk about him to other people but I would never allow myself to feel any emotion while I did. I was hanging onto control.'

'At the same time, I had so many crazy dreams – I had animals to look after that died, I was meant to keep jewellery safe and lost it, I had a garden that wouldn't grow anything – all loss and failure dreams. Even though Shane didn't come into my dreams, when I opened my eyes he filled my mind. Gradually, that tidal wave of loss became easier to be with.'

'I went to see a counsellor, too. Everyone is different so has uniquely different ways to heal. I believe the greatest gift counsellors can give is that they listen without getting emotional about your experiences. This is massively helpful.'

'If you talk to somebody close to you about tragic events, their love and care shows in the pain on their face. When I tried to talk to Mum about my brother Pete's death, I worried how she felt and that was an additional problem – her hurting. I did not want her to feel my pain.'

'When you need to talk, counsellors provide the opportunity to off-load without feeling guilty. That said, there will always be some part of your subconscious that does not want to be laid bare to another human being, and that's where your subconscious takes over and deals with it in the dream state.'

Roz

'You said that once you identify the emotion under a nightmare, it stops. I think the emotion under my dreams might be anger. My boyfriend Mark has been really badly treated by a man he worked for and I wake up feeling cross and powerless on his behalf.'

Mia

'You love Mark and want to take his pain away, but you also know it's a situation he must deal with for his own self-respect – and you wouldn't rob him of that, so that leaves you feeling frustrated.'

'We can have the same feeling for children who are being bullied at school. A major part of us wants to go to the school and be horrible to whoever is picking on our cub, but the sensible side of us knows that we do our children a far better service by taking one step back and teaching them the skills to deal with the situation for themselves.'

'You're right, Roz – by connecting your dreams with what you're really feeling, the dreams should calm and fade away. Eric has taught me that if we try to keep the past locked away and don't look at it or address it, then it keeps knocking and interfering with the now in our life.'

'When I became divorced and was on my own with my children Shane and Tanya, I didn't know why I still felt scared. I was in a cottage in the country and I had my freedom – it was something that I had wanted for at least 10 years and yet it was as if I was still waiting for something bad to happen. I couldn't relax into what I had, I couldn't enjoy it.'

'You'd think, having Eric around, I'd turn to him immediately, but he is usually my last port of call. First, I usually try to run away from the problem by keeping my mind as busy as possible. But it never works for very long.'

'Early one morning, I woke before anyone else. I was in the kitchen of the new cottage and the Rayburn was still glowing from the night before. Suddenly, I had an enormous lump in my throat. I had everything that I'd dreamed of for so long – so why did I feel so dreadful?'

'I was sitting at the kitchen table and I put my head in my hands. Without thinking about it, I said, "Oh Eric, what am I going to do?" It was an instinctive groan rather than a question, but Eric was immediately clear in my mind.'

'"I think it's about time you looked at the situation properly, don't you?"'

'Yeah, like how?'

'"Why do you think people like listening to comedians and hearing funny stories?"'

'Because they're funny.'

'"Of course they're funny, but it's the emotion they get from the stories. Laughter is food for the soul."'

'I couldn't see where this was going, but I agreed with him that this was obvious.'

'Eric said, "It is the same with all emotions, be they negative or positive – they have an effect on the soul. You can't dam them up, you can't stop the flow. You must experience them and let them move on. Just as laughter can come and go, so should pain."'

'"The problems start when we don't let pain flood over us. We try to block it, hide from it, anything rather than let it touch us. But it won't go anywhere else. It stays there waiting until you experience it."'

'"You left your husband and hoped that you left your emotions behind with him, but you can't do that. They're your emotions. They're what make you who you are. You have to experience them and accept them, then you can stand away from them."'

'How can I do that?'

'By this time, I had tears streaming down my face. I knew what Eric was saying was true. I thought by leaving my abusive husband, Andy, I'd leave the angst behind too. But it was still with me – nothing had changed because the feelings were still inside me.'

'Living with Andy, I'd lost myself. I didn't know who I was, what I wanted, where I wanted to be going – I didn't even know what food I wanted to eat, what music I liked to hear. All that had mattered had been surviving. I had been keeping my emotions in check for so long, I didn't even realize I was still doing it.'

'Eric waited patiently while I went through the emotions and felt them as they surfaced – terror, shame, a sense of having no control over my life. As I sat at the table, the emotions swamped me and I sobbed. I thought I'd never feel better but gradually I stopped crying and I started to calm down. I felt lighter, as if a great physical weight had been lifted off me – the weight of all those unfelt feelings.'

'"That was good for you," Eric said. "Now, for the future, you don't have to dam your emotions. Life is full of stress but there are ways of dealing with it. Emotions are energies. What you need to do is step apart from your emotions and see them as an energy of their own. See them, feel them and let them pass through you."'

'Eric showed me a visualization technique to help me see that the emotions aren't the soul, they are just experiences that the spirit goes through. I've used the technique countless times since that day and it's never failed to help me. Would you like to try it?'

Roz

I was still feeling incensed by the way Mark had been treated by his employer. I could see Mia's point. I would be of more help to Mark if I was less churned up. I thought it was a great idea to distance myself from my emotions.

Mia

'Get into a comfortable position, close your eyes, sigh and drop. Go into the zone, using whatever technique you are comfortable with. Now visualize yourself standing in a very fast-flowing stream. The stream is full of thick swirling colours that represent your emotions. The stream is moving very fast and all the colours are bashing against your legs.'

'Give each colour a situation that's causing you pain. Mark's employer could be one colour. Your finances could be another colour. Even the housework could be another colour. Anything that causes you stress, give it a colour and acknowledge it hitting and splashing up against you.'

'The stream has to be deep enough for you to feel the pressure of the water. Thigh level is good. The idea is that you are fighting to keep on your feet and the water is trying to topple you.'

Roz

It took a while but, finally, I got the image of the stream.

'I've got my feet apart and the water is rushing, but I haven't got any colours.'

Mia

'Okay, you're just about staying upright against the flow of the water, then a coloured oil slick comes rushing towards you.'

Roz

'I am seeing olive green. I didn't expect that – it's so subtle. I thought I'd see primary colours like red and blue.'

Mia

'It's interesting that you're automatically seeing a dark, sludgy colour. It represents a dark, sludgy feeling. What do you think this colour represents?'

Roz

'Mark's work situation – the fact that he has been so used.'

Mia

'As you visualize the colour coming towards you, it is important you believe that all your emotion and angst about the situation is part of the colour. Give it life and power. Concentrate on that colour; what is it doing?'

Roz

'It's splashing all over me and coating my skin.'

Mia

'Visualize it clearing away. There is clean water coming. You are still holding your balance. Now another colour should come.'

Roz

'Dark, liver-coloured red.'

Mia

'What do you think that is?'

Roz

'My finances.'

Mia

'That makes sense. Because you're a vegetarian, you don't like to look at blood, liver or anything to do with dead animal parts. So you don't look at your finances properly and hope they somehow get mysteriously sorted out. See that colour coming towards you, let the image flow and see what it does.'

Roz

'The same thing, but perhaps with a little less power. It's splashing rather than covering me.'

Mia

'Clean water is coming. Once you have the clear water again, wait for the colour.'

Roz

'Mustard yellow. It's the housework I haven't done.'

Mia

'The colour that we don't want our paint work to be. Let it come towards you and see what happens.'

Roz

'The mustard yellow is just coating my legs as it floats by. The truth is, most of the time I don't really care if the housework gets done or not.'

Mia

'Well done, Roz. You analyzed the last colour yourself. The energy and power behind the colour was different. It also showed you which situations were affecting you the most.'

'Now I want you to step out of the stream and sit on the bank. Imagine it is wonderful, lush and mossy. It is a place of calm and serenity. You are totally safe. The stream has all three colours covering the top of the water. Watch the colours jostle each other and carry on down the stream.'

'This is life, it will always be busy, fast and full of emotions, but you can step outside. Emotions don't always have to be buffeting you and clinging to you. All the colours and emotions are still there, but you are sitting apart from them. Acknowledge that, even though you have these emotions, they don't have to drown you, they will pass by.'

'The key here is that the power of those colours doesn't lessen when you get on the bank. It's just that they can't touch you. Whenever you feel overwhelmed by life, visualize yourself in the stream, bring forth the colours, then rest on the bank. All you need to do is go into the zone. It will help you all through your life.'

'By the way, well done Roz. For the first time you used visualization techniques to get information from the zone. Up until now, all the images you've seen have been random with no reference to any specific situation – be it your life or anyone else's. But when I asked you to build the image of the stream and the colours and the river-bank, once you had that image in your mind, without me having to tell you, the colours took on a life of their own.'

'Each emotion gave itself strength and colour, showing you its effect on your life. And each appeared in its order of importance to you.'

Roz

'I think it's true that I didn't choose the colours – they're not colours that appeal to me.'

Mia

'You also didn't choose their power – the amount they pushed against and covered you. Do you agree?'

Roz

'The colours certainly seemed to have a life of their own, but I can't be sure it wasn't my imagination playing around.'

Mia

'That dilemma will always be with you. Even when I've done a really good reading, when the client leaves, doubt sometimes creeps in. If I've said something outrageous or seen a change the client can't relate to or believe in, it can shake my belief. It's only after years of receiving confirmation about my psychic ability, that I've learned to discard the worry, and have faith.'

'It's good that your insecurity is there. The best psychics in the world are unconfident. They are "sensitives" – sensitives are not bullyish or full of themselves – they are gentle people. They often have low self-esteem and suffer from anxiety and nerves. Very often they have experienced a trauma that has deepened their understanding of life. It is that sensitivity, though, that allows them to ride the zone easier than others. It's only with time, practice, trust and belief that your self-doubt will lessen. In time, it won't have such a hold on you.'

'The most exciting thing about the river image is that you deciphered that last colour as it came towards you. You told me that housework wasn't a big deal to you – as you were seeing the image you were telling me what it meant. You were just chatting, you didn't realize you were doing it. You got psychic information and interpreted it correctly.'

Roz

I was mildly irritated. Mia was always so convinced that my thoughts came from psychic information.

'Of course I knew what the colours meant – they were about me.'

Mia

'Yes, but if I'd told you to prioritize the negative emotions in your life, you'd have said they were all muddled. The psychic side of you gave you additional, clearer information via the subtle shades of colour, the order they came and the force with which they hit your legs.'

'The wonderful thing about psychic information is that, when you see it, it seems so obvious – it's like old information, something you've always known. I'm convinced the imagery gave you added information and showed you how these emotions are affecting your life.'

'Visual images in your mind are the tools you will work with as a psychic. Just as a carpenter uses a saw and a painter uses a brush, you will use visualization techniques. You are ready to work in the zone as a psychic does.'

Roz

'What – after one dream and sitting with you for a few hours using my imagination … I'm not – I can't be.'

Mia

'You were working psychically just now. You went into the zone and used visualization techniques to get information. That is exactly what I do every time I do a reading. There is no certificate, no magical moment when you go from being non-psychic to psychic.'

'Now you've found the zone, you'll never lose it. And even if this thought scares you: every time you go into the zone, you are working as a psychic. The only thing we don't know is how far you can get – how clearly you can see. And we don't know how good you will be at deciphering images into meaning. That's what the next teachings will be about.'

Chapter 16

Working in the Zone

Mia

In bed that night, I found it hard to sleep. I was feeling annoyed at myself. I'd made another grand statement. Roz was able to use visualization techniques and see random images, but how the hell was I going to turn that into the tools of a working psychic? The only reference I had, was the way I worked. I hoped that would be enough.

The next day, at Roz's cottage, I started to break down what I do in a reading, and I explained how I take a thread of the person into the zone with me.

'I start by making eye contact with my client. Remember, the eyes really are the window to the soul. Learning to look through that window and see the real person is the true beginning of clairvoyance. We may be able to build walls around ourselves – in our mannerisms, our speech, our clothes – but the eyes reveal our essential selves. Once I've locked into their eyes, I tell myself over and over: "I know you, I know you, I know you." It's like I'm trying to step inside their skin and link into their essence.'

'Then I explain what I am going to do. I say, "I'll start with a health scan, go into your aura and personality, go in to your finances, work, relationships and then scan out. All the time I'm talking, I try to keep eye contact."'

'By the time I've finished my explanation and looked away, I am ready to begin. Throughout the rest of the reading, I look over the person's shoulder, as if into the distance. Once the reading has started, it is of no concern to me whether they agree with what I'm saying or not. I am committed to the reading – to what I'm picking up with my psychic antenna – so their facial expressions would be a distraction.'

'Each area of the reading has its own visual imagery that helps me to work in that field. With the health scan, for instance, I look at the person opposite me and visualize a line of light above their head. Once I can see it clearly, I believe it has a life of its own. Then I sit back and watch the line of light descend through the client's body.'

'If there is a problem, the line of light stops and I get a flash image of a colour. Over the years, I have learned to decipher the colours. For example, as I'm looking at you now, the line of white light is flickering over your eyes with bits of pink. Pink, to me, is irritation – that's the way I interpret that colour. This just means that your eyes are tired and sore.'

'Even though the images come and go very quickly, I can retrieve them to examine them more closely. It's like building blocks, you use your first images to get more.'

'For instance, I might start with a flash of pink on your shoulder. I recall that image and let it sit in my mind's eye. After a little while, I will get another flash – perhaps of bone against gristle – or I will get a feeling. If I feel a flutter of irritation, then I know the problem is just a mild nuisance. If I get an anxiety with it, that alerts me that there could be a more serious problem with the shoulder.'

'I rely on the colours red and pink in a health reading. If I see a flash of red, that is real illness, true pain. Deepest red is the most worrying, lightest pink is the least. There are many shades in between.'

'I also notice how long the image takes to go away in my mind – that's a rough indicator of how long it will take to get better. If the problem is major, I get visual images that give me extra information. If I see a cancerous tumour it slowly rotates and comes towards me so I can see its size, position and strength. I'm not medically trained, but if I see tendrils on it, I know that it's spreading.'

'This is where the real art of being a psychic comes in. When you first start to read psychically, it's easy to get excited by the clarity of the pictures. But what's more important is the reason you are being shown those pictures.'

'Your job as a psychic is not to show the client how clever you are by picking it up, but to help them through it. You acknowledge what they're going through, you may even say it is going to get worse before it gets better. But you never say that it won't get better. The reason for receiving the information is to get the person to the doctor in the gentlest way possible. There's no benefit in making it into a drama and freaking them out.'

Roz

'What do you do if you see something bad happening to someone in the future?'

Mia

'Remember, it's only through emotional challenges that the soul can grow. Also, we can't change the things in life that are meant to be. But if I see something negative in someone's future, I am very careful about the details I reveal. I give the person enough clues to show them later, when they are going through the situation, that I picked up on it during the reading. That way, they can take comfort that the positive information I gave them is also real.'

'The purpose of a reading is to give the soul the energy to see it through. No matter what terrible thing we come up against, the importance lies in how we deal with the experience. And your job is to give the client hope.'

Roz
'Even if they are going to die?'

Mia
'Death is not the catastrophe that society thinks it is. I remember a regular client who'd been coming to see me for five years. She'd battled breast cancer and was in remission when she came on a sunny day in June.'

'My first impression of her was that it was lovely to see her so happy and full of life. But when I opened up and went into the zone, I saw images of cancerous tumours everywhere. I was horrified. I realized she was going to die. She was a young mum; she had kids and a zest for life that few people have.'

'I also realized, in almost the same instant, that I would never give her such an important reading as the one I was about to give her. I couldn't allow my emotions to interfere with the help that was needed. She knew I was doing the health scan and she said: "You haven't said anything."'

'"Well you know I like to tell the truth," I said, "and life doesn't always run smoothly. It looks like the cancer is coming back and I do know you'll be going into hospital as an outpatient, maybe more than that."'

'Her face fell. "But I'm in remission. I only had the blood test two weeks ago."'

'I felt as if I was her enemy. Everything in me wanted to say: "It will be fine, it won't come back, don't worry." But I knew that, when the going got rough, this would be of no help to her. I remember reaching across the table and holding her hand and saying, "Hey, you've been here before. And you were really negative then. Look at you now. Forewarned is forearmed."'

'I tried to keep it upbeat. I told her that she'd have a grotty winter and she'd be really tested. But I promised her, after Christmas, everything would be okay and she wouldn't be stressed about her health. I looked her in the eye and said, "I promise". I felt dreadful when she said, "You've always been right before."'

'They buried her early in the New Year. I didn't know until her sisters came to see me. They'd found the taped recording of the reading I'd given her. They told me that she'd gained a lot from the reading and that, when she was at her sickest, she often listened to the tape.'

'Although the cancer coming back had been a terrible blow, the reading gave her hope. She died, sure of an afterlife where she would be at peace and reunited with her loved ones.'

Roz

'So the real art of being a psychic is not how clever you are at getting the information, but how clever you are at giving it.'

Mia

'That's it. I believe that getting the information is only forty percent of the job. The way you give the information is the other sixty. When you become better at being psychic, the human side of you will get excited. You'll want to say everything you get, but the spiritual side has to only work from a place of parental love. You'll be tested again and again.'

'No matter what the age of the person you're talking to, you must work and care for them as you would your own child. And as we don't scare our children, so we never scare those we read for. A reading is a place of honour, not a theatrical stage.'

'Now let's carry on with analyzing the rest of the reading. After the health scan, I go into reading the personality. I see and acknowledge the person's aura and I wait for colours, either in their aura or in my mind's eye.'

'The basic colours I get are blue, green, brown, pink, silver, gold and occasionally purple. Each means a different personality trait or emotion. For most psychics, flashes of colour are the most easily accessible form of information.'

'Blue is the people colour, the caring, social, colour. It can range from the lightest blue – where I would think someone is being superficial – to the deepest of blues which shows an old soul – a warm, caring person.'

'Purple is an off-shoot of blue. If I see purple, somebody is an active healer – definitely. A healer of minds or of bodies. Now imagine all the blue shades in between – you have to use your gut instinct to decipher what they mean.'

'Green is earth, practical. Light green means somebody is enthusiastic, energetic and motivated. Darkest green means the person doesn't like changes, they are entrenched and pedantic. Again you have to interpret every shade in between.'

'Brown is the colour of depression, it means that things have been heavy for the person. Lightest brown could mean an irritating week or day, deepest brown is a deep depression.'

'Pink is stress, anxiety. I usually see pink in little flutters of colour which tell me that anxiety is coming. (Whereas brown represents a situation that has passed or that is). The more pink there is, the more anxiety.'

'Silver is the colour of the untrained psychic – someone who has a natural aptitude but is not using it properly. Gold is the highest colour of all – the sign that someone is in touch with their spirituality.'

'From these quick flashes of colour, I am building a total personality profile. And, all the time I'm talking, I am building my confidence and my belief that I know this person.'

Roz

'Do you remember the dreams I had that told you I was psychic

– the dreams where my guide told me that aura colours were iridescent like the colours in a rock crystal I had? I've hunted high and low for that crystal but I never found it. I think I have given it away. Anyway, in the end, last week, I bought another one. If my guide really did refer me to it for advice on auras I thought I better follow it up.'

Mia
'What colour is your crystal?'

Roz
'The same as the one I lost, pinky purple.'

Mia
'And what do those colours represent?'

Roz
'Stress and healing.'

Mia
'I think that's quite apt don't you?'

Taking the tiny rock crystal from Roz, I consulted Eric.

'Eric says, "You were drawn to buying the crystal in the first place because it is the same colours that are in your aura. Your guide brought it into your dream for two reasons. Firstly to show you the iridescent nature of aura colours. Secondly, to work with something concrete and tangible – something you had had in your possession – that had the same colours as your own aura."'

Chapter 17

The Relationship Room

Mia

'Apart from the health scan, the relationship reading is what people are most interested in and it's a vital part of any reading.'

'With relationship readings, I visualize an empty room and then I put an image of the person I'm reading for in the room. Then, as before, I sit back and wait to see what will happen. For instance, I am putting you in the room but you keep moving around busily. Now I see your boyfriend, Mark, a couple of feet away from you, watching you with his arms crossed and a smile on his face. This is interesting because I thought you were the calm one in the relationship but I'm being shown that it is the other way around.'

'The image tells me that you're giving yourself stress needlessly – thinking you need to fiddle around with things and work on bits of the relationship to keep it safe. But Mark knows your relationship doesn't need fussing over. He's strong, stable and smiling at you with love.'

'Stop worrying about what might be and what problems could arise and enjoy the relationship. The way he's smiling at your busyness, tells me that he thinks your idiosyncrasies are cute – he may not understand them but he loves you all the more for them.'

Roz

As usual, torn between being impressed or picky, I chose the latter.

'And what about the fact he's got his arms crossed? What does that mean?'

Mia

'He's waiting for you to stop faffing around and he's there when you're ready to take it to the next stage.'

Roz

I trusted Mark implicitly. Nevertheless, I couldn't help asking the next question.

'If he was having an affair, what would you have seen?'

Mia

'A third person in the room. I always wait to see where this person goes before I say anything. If they move towards the partner of the person I'm reading for and stand close, there is an affair going on.'

'If the third person appears and then dissolves without moving, I know that the client has anxieties about being betrayed. The strength of that fear can be the same as if it was real, and it is the fear which makes the third figure manifest.'

Roz

'And if there was an affair going on, would you tell the client?'

Mia

'I used to, but I've realized that there is more to it than that. I don't condone infidelity but it takes many forms. A partner may have a brief fling once in a whole marriage and bitterly regret it. In other words, I can't always tell if the affair is going to destroy the partnership or not.'

'The other thing I have to take into account is that some peo-ple need to know what is going on – and others don't. I take each case individually but I always ensure that truth is the basis of everything I say. I give clues – for example I might mention the third person's name or I might say: 'You're going to be re-evalu-ating your relationship soon.'

'If the person is ready for the information they will see it or ask more questions. If they can't cope, then the clues will pass them by. So I judge the temperature, I try to be subtle and I let the person I'm reading for give me an indication as to whether they want the whole truth or not.'

Roz

'It sounds very cloak and dagger. Isn't it better to be straight?'

Mia

'I never mislead people. Whatever they decide to make of the information I give them, when they listen to the tape at a future date and events have come to pass, they'll know that I knew.'

Roz

'Why don't you just tell them? If my partner was being unfaith-ful, I'd want to know.'

Mia

'I remember doing that in my early years. Not only did I tell a woman that her husband was having an affair, I gave her the woman's name and said it was a friend of hers. Three hours later, her husband was hammering on my door saying, "How dare you tell my wife I'm being unfaithful."'

'I opened the front door, trying to be calm. In my naivete, I said: "But you are having an affair."'

'Suddenly his anger turned to grief. His voice had a catch in it as he told me, "It's finished. I was trying to save my marriage, now she'll never forgive me."'

'I realized then that I should not have interfered. If I had just said: "That friend isn't such a great friend", they could have been happy for another 30 years. A bit of me was showing off. I played God and I shouldn't have. Now my objective – as with the health scan – is very simple: the person has got a problem, encourage them to address it.'

'Working as a psychic you learn that people can't always hear the truth. Say you're doing a reading for a woman whose husband has just left her. At that moment in time, the only thing she wants to hear is that her husband is coming back. You know it's not going to happen but you do know that she'll be in love with some-body else in, say, nine months time – and happier than she's been for years. But you can't give that information in a crude way.'

'Most people live in the present – they think how they're feel-ing now is how they are always going to feel. Even though they can accept their moods have changed many times in the past week – or day or hour – they find it hard to accept that their pain and longing will ever go away.'

'So you say: "I'm not sure if your husband is coming back but I do know for sure that in nine months time, you'll be totally in love and in a relationship that makes you very happy. This could be your husband or it could be somebody new."'

'The most likely response to this is: "Oh, it's definitely my hus-band because I couldn't love anyone else." By the time she leaves, she will have convinced herself you said that. It's not until after the event and she listens to the tape, that she'll realize you did tell the truth but in a way that she could cope with at that point in her life.'

'Each situation must be judged and handled differently. The whole point is to comfort the person with your knowledge. That is the reason for getting the information, that is the essential thing.'

Roz

'Is there such a thing as a soul mate?'

Mia

'The truth is, you don't have just one soul mate. You could have four or five in a lifetime – and they don't have to be lovers, they could be your best friend or a member of your family. There is no way of telling how long they will be in your life. It may be only for a couple of years or a lifetime. But, whoever they are, when you meet them, there is always a feeling of recognition. This is because you have met before. They are your "soul friends", the ones you know at "home", the ones with whom you discuss all the experiences you've been through in this lifetime. It is only once you are "home" that your memory of them is reawakened.'

'The other question that people often ask me is: "How do I know that the relationship I am in is going to last?" You don't. You're not meant to know. The love and happiness we experience in romantic relationships is like a holiday for the soul. When you fall in love, the world is a beautiful place. Everything sparkles with life and colour. Your spirit soars. This is all food for the soul. Rest and play are as important for your soul as the times of learning and growth.'

'If you love for 10 days or for 10 years, it is always meant to be, and you should enter into it bravely and enjoy it for what it is. It takes courage to let your defences down and fall in love. True love is unconditional and non-judgemental, which is why parental love is the nearest we get to it on Earth. To fall truly in love one must do so without guarantees.'

Roz

'So people fall out of love because they are meant to move on?'

Mia

'Yes. Life is a journey not a destination. All we can be certain of is that things change. All relationships will go through times of grief – there'll be times when your partner irritates you. That's natural. It's only when you no longer want their company that you know it's reached a natural end. It may not always be for ever – there may be a point when you get back together – but for now it's finished. Your paths are meant to go in different directions at that point.'

'Having said this, some people do find the love of their lives and stay with them until they die. The likelihood is that they are young souls, given one person to go through life with, as a buffer against their other life experiences.'

Roz

'There are times when you should fight for a relationship and times when you need to let it go. How can you tell what is the right thing to do?'

Mia

'We all know deep in our hearts when it is right and when it is wrong. I once gave a reading to a woman who had fallen in love with a man in her office. Even though she had never even spoken to him properly, her feelings for this man were taking over her life. She couldn't eat or sleep and she thought about him all the time.'

'By doing this she was stuck in a loop and creating a pause in her life, like a time bubble. I explained that she had to push for-ward – either by telling him how she felt, or by deciding to let it go and move on. If she told him and he felt the same way, they could start a relationship. If not, she needed to accept reality and start healing herself.'

'In time, she started to go out again and see her friends, meet new people, and have fun. A couple of months later, she met another man and the pain of that unrequited love was forgotten. She had burst the bubble.'

'The pain of unrequited love is up there in the top ten of hard life lessons. To love someone who does not feel the same as you can be devastating. I have seen this painful situation in many different forms in my work as a clairvoyant, but it is hard to show someone the life lesson under the pain – I always know that it is meant to be. Once you have established that the other person does not want to be in a relationship with you, you must step back and let them walk their own path. No one can force another to love them – we cannot force something that isn't real. The important thing is to be brave and not put your life on hold. Push your life forward.'

'To truly love someone means that you want the best for them, regardless of your own desires. Unrequited love is about facing your aloneness. Not getting what you want reinforces a sense of loneliness. But one of life's major lessons is learning to be alone and enjoy your own company. It's at these times that we develop our spirituality and psychic awareness.'

Roz
'Some people keep having disastrous relationships over and over. Is it because they are also stuck in a loop?'

Mia
'That's right, because they won't learn their lesson. When you repeatedly find yourself in a bad relationship, the only way to break the cycle is to stop it as soon as it starts to go wrong. Underneath it all, people caught in this loop don't feel they have

the right to be treated well. Because they don't feel enough respect for themselves, they will often make excuses for their partner – each time they are treated badly, they allow the goalposts to be shifted a little further apart. But everyone is entitled to respect within a relationship. Everybody owes it to their complete self to acknowledge their absolute right to be treated well by others.'

'The rest of the reading is based around finances and work. For finances, I visualize a graph with ten squares up and ten across, then I put a line on it, sit back and wait to see where it goes. If it goes up, things are good. If the line plummets, then financial caution is advised.'

'With work, I use a white room, just as with the relationship reading. The difference is I tell myself I am looking for information about work. I always finish every reading on a "floater". Here I go into the zone, but I am so immersed in the other person's life now that I don't need any structure. I wait for random images to come and I just tell them as I see them – even when they seem ridiculous.'

'At the end of the reading, I ask the person if they have any questions. Most times, I can go back to something I have seen during the reading and wait for it to expand. So if they ask: "Will I get the new job I applied for?" I go back to the work visual, remember what I saw and see if there is a sense of new beginnings or disappointment.'

'I always finish on an upbeat note. You should always leave them feeling better than when they came in.'

Roz
'A lot of people think the real proof of being a psychic would be winning the lottery by predicting the numbers. Could you get that sort of information if you wanted to?'

Mia

'You've hit on one of the questions I get asked the most: "What are next week's lottery numbers?"'

'It doesn't work like that. The only psychic feedback you can get on the future is information that has no emotional impact on you personally. Money is a hugely emotional issue for almost everyone. Of course, there's a part of me that would like the lottery numbers very much, but now I don't even try as it would be wrong.'

'There have only been a few times when something like that has worked for me. The first was when I won at bingo with my mum. It was just after my brother Pete had died and the whole family was totally broke. One day, while I was putting flowers on Pete's grave, an image of me and Mum at bingo suddenly flashed into my mind. I only had £3 in my purse, but we went anyway. Later that evening, we came out of Sheerness Club with the National Prize of £55,000. It made me so happy that my instinct helped me provide my family with some of the money that they needed. "It's a gift from Pete", Mum said.'

'Another time I struck lucky, was just after I had met one of my friends, Matthew. When I first knew him, he didn't believe in any of "that psychic stuff" at all. Matthew was a very astute businessman. Logical and practical, he only believed what he could see with his own eyes. Within a couple of days of meeting me, he was mischievously making fun of what I did.'

'"OK, Mia. If you really are a psychic, tell me the winner of tomorrow's Derby."'

'Matthew brought out a long list of all the horses taking part in the race and slapped it down on the table in front of me. My eyes scoured the list of names, until one seemed to jump out at me, as if it was in bolder print than the others. "That one," I said.'

'"Alright then, if that one wins you can use my spare office for your work."'

'The next day my horse won and I got my office. For the next three weeks, Matthew rushed into my office every day with lists of horses' names, eager for me to pick another winner. He was quite prepared to give the money to charity, but he was fascinated to see if I could do it again. Unfortunately, I couldn't. I now think that I was just meant to become friends with Matthew and get the office I needed for my work. Both the Derby and the bingo win had been a case of the universe allowing my psychic abilities to help me out for a good reason. But these pieces of good fortune had come to me, I had not gone looking for them.'

'Over the last few years, there have been a number of occasions when I've had a lot of financial worries. In my early days of being psychic I sometimes asked Eric if he could give me the lottery numbers or the football results, just to help me through a difficult period. My argument was that if I didn't have to worry about money, I could concentrate all my energies on my work. Eric's answer has always been the same: "Why should you be helped and others not?"'

'Whenever we had this discussion, I got pictures in my head of people suffering – people denied warmth, shelter, food. If there was one miracle that could happen on that day, then I really wasn't at the front of the queue for deserving causes.'

'The work I do is in addition to dealing with life, not instead of it. There's no cosy psychic bubble wrapped around me. Even if I wanted to, I can't make my own life comfortable by using my predictions to conveniently steer me through life's problems. I still have to worry about the bills, my family, health issues. That will never change, and that's how it should be.'

Roz
'My next question is what's the timing on all the information you get? How do you know whether it's about the past, present or future?'

Mia

'That is the most difficult question of all. I have to say, that in all the cases where I've been able to follow up with a client, I have never been wrong on the events that are going to happen to them, but sometimes my timing is off. The hardest skill for any psychic to learn is time. The only advice I can give you is that you will get to learn that the past feels like it was, has been, has already come to pass. Now feels like it is happening *now*. And the future has a slight uncertainty about it, a feeling of being not quite sure.'

'The emotional changes are so slight that, twenty years down the line, I still sometimes get it wrong. It only comes with practice. And, as Eric always tells me: "Have faith."'

Roz

There was so much to learn, so much to remember. Being a psychic was a huge responsibility. What if I got it horribly wrong?

'Mia, you really think I'm ready to do this work?'

Mia

'You're ready to get the information – but whether you give it clumsily or with compassion, is down to you. You will get better with practice, but your basic personality will define your bedside manner.'

'The easiest thing to start with is an emotional reading. Everything is based around emotions and the way someone is feeling is the easiest to read. When I started out, I always began a reading with a person's emotions and personality because, once I had that, I could get a handle on their life. It made the rest easier to see.'

'Let's take a little look at emotions. I'd like you to think back over the last ten years in your life and tell me three occasions that made you happy and three that made you sad, distressed or annoyed. Which ones are the easiest to remember?'

Roz

'The hard times – losing my beloved cat Ludwig, having a crappy relationship and being in a crash where my car was written off. The happy times all seem to be more recent.'

Mia

'Okay, give me three happy times that happened more than a year ago.'

Roz

'That is harder. My novels being published, my first holiday with Mark ...'

Mia

'Even though you can't remember them, there were thousands of times that you laughed, danced and partied, met new people, had new experiences. It's not unbalanced, it's just a fact of life. Happiness and pleasure are like holidays for the soul but you don't learn much when you're happy. That's why sad times have a deeper impact.'

'Okay, you've had a little look at emotions, now it's time to choose a visual aid. You need a space onto which images can appear. That's why I use a room for both relationship and work readings.'

'If you don't like the idea of the room, you can go back to the blackboard or a TV screen or a stage, a meadow clearing, a beach. It is limitless. It took me months to find images that worked for me. You need to find images that you're comfortable with and that make sense to you. Your relationship room could be a giant empty heart surrounded with cupids, all pink and fluffy. It could be a room or even a stage. It doesn't matter what image you use, as long as you are clear that the image represents relationships.'

'Also, once you find an image, you need to stick to it and use it over and over again. That way, your sixth sense gets familiar with the image and makes it easier and clearer for you to get the information.'

Roz
'I like the idea of the room, but am I just copying you? Should I be trying to come up with something new, just for me?'

Mia
'I've tried so many different images but rooms work for me because they provide an empty space for details to come in. There can be furniture, lighting, temperature, ornaments – all of which give information about what's going on.'

'So I think it's good to visualize a room, but start with it completely blank and empty – try not to even think of the walls, just know that they are there.'

'Okay, let's have a practice run. Think of a friend that you haven't seen for a little while. Now sit comfortably, close your eyes, sigh and drop. Visualize the empty room.'

Roz
'If it's empty and it's got no walls, what am I seeing?'

Mia
'Give it white walls, ceiling and floor. Whenever you use a room as a visualization tool, give it a doorway so that people and situations can come in and go out.'

Roz
'Okay, I've got a very basic white room, Mia.'

Mia

'I want you to think of your friend, remember the way she stands and put her in that position in the middle of the room. You may think you have the visual strongly but you have to build it. The colour, length and texture of her hair – remember it and look at it.'

'The shape of her eyebrows, the colour of her eyes. The eyes are really important, unique to each person. Just the eyes alone can tell you everything.'

'Now remember her mouth when she's smiling and when she's not.'

Roz

'Why are the details so important?'

Mia

'Remembering her physically will strengthen the psychic link. Now visualize the length and shape of her neck, her shoulders – are they rounded, square, broad, thin? Her clothes should be ones that you are familiar with.'

'Her hands – are they worn and rough or soft? Are the nails long and cared for or bitten and chewed? Is she wearing rings and bracelets?'

'Now sit back and look again, the image should be stronger.'

Roz

'Yes, I can see her clearly.'

Mia

'Now let go and observe what happens.'

Roz

'I can see the bits of her – her mouth, eyes, hands – but I can't keep the whole image there.'

Mia

'That's okay, once you've reaffirmed your memory, an outline or silhouette is enough.'

Roz

'That's strange, I'm seeing the silhouette pat a dog. She doesn't really like pets.'

Mia

'Don't analyze it and don't get involved emotionally, just look.'

Roz

'Maybe something to do with a ring, I can see her fiddling with a ring on her finger.'

Mia

'Your mind will try to make the picture whole and bring other things in to make sense of it. Keep making yourself step back, let it go again, don't analyze it.'

Roz

'Now I think the room has turned into her living room at home because I can see her back garden through the window. I've lost the picture. I can't see anything now.'

Mia

'That's great for a first time. Open your eyes and let's talk. Three images: a dog, fiddling with her hands and looking out through a window. Now, what do you reckon the dog meant?'

Roz

'That someone has asked her to look after their dog and she has reluctantly agreed.'

Mia

'So what's the basic emotion behind that?'

Roz

'Reluctance.'

Mia

'So that was the message from the image. She feels she's been manoeuvred into a situation that she can't get out of. She's also not voicing her opinions because she's patting the dog and pretending it's okay.'

'When you said she was fiddling with a ring on her finger, your hand instinctively went to the marriage finger. That would tell me that the situation is uncomfortable and is based around relationships.'

'Last, looking out to the garden through the window, what do you think that represents? Did you feel any traces of your friend's emotion when you were looking out through the window?'

Roz

It was hard to separate my feelings from my friends.

'I don't know, Mia. What do you think?'

Mia

'To me, the window signifies being hemmed in. You know your friend's garden, yet you weren't transported to the garden, you just saw it through a window. Once again, the feeling is of being trapped.'

'Working in the zone, you can't analyze what you see, you just see. The two stages are separate: the gathering and the deciphering. If you try to make sense of what you're seeing while you're in the zone, you'll either lose the image or your imagination will take over.'

'When I'm giving a reading, I see an image, gather information about it, analyze it, then give the information. For instance, if your friend had been sitting opposite me and I'd seen those three symbols, I wouldn't tell her the images, they would be of no use to her.'

'All I would say is: "You're feeling pressured, you're not in control of your life at the moment. You feel hemmed in. There's a need to get out of a situation, a need for freedom. Don't let relationships rule you. Keep your identity within them."'

'You have crossed the biggest barrier – from floating aimlessly in the zone to honing in on other people and receiving information concerning their lives. The next step is to hold the images you get for longer. Wait for feeling to come with them. That way you will get more information.'

'As you practise, you'll get more detail from each symbol. It can be very subtle. You might feel or sense something, you may see colours, some things may be in shadow or bright light. There's more information in one "flash" than you can imagine. The longer you hold the image, the more information you'll get.'

'You can stop, write down what you've seen and then bring the image back and let it continue. By the way, a word of advice – this technique can't be used to spy on boyfriends or workmates. You only get a true link if your intention is pure.'

'I'd like you to make a note of the symbols you saw and, when you speak to your friend, ask her how she's feeling. Afterwards go back to the symbols, and you'll start to learn the way that your subconscious is communicating with you. Remember: the more you trust, the more accurate you will be.'

Roz

'I'll run the pictures past my friend because it's an exercise. But I think if I do find out I have psychic powers, I'll keep it to myself. I'm not sure I could handle that role. I don't want to be on show.'

Mia

'Being psychic is not about learning small individual tricks or putting on a performance, it is about being yourself. It is important to believe in yourself and let others know you believe in what you do. It doesn't matter if people approve of you or disapprove; what is important is how you feel about yourself. Never apologize for who you are.'

'When I started working, I did so as a closet psychic. If people didn't need to know I had a gift, I didn't tell them. I kept it quiet because people's reactions were always strong. It was either confrontation – people telling me they didn't believe and wanting me to know why – or people were into it and wanted something from me.'

'The day I decided to come out of the closet, I'd been working during the day and went to pick my daughter Tanya up from school. She was ten and attending the convent in Sittingbourne. While I was waiting in the playground, three of the other mothers walked over and introduced themselves. We were chatting about the school when one asked, "What is it you do for a living?"'

'They were Catholic mothers. When I said, "I work as a psychic", it was like chucking a bucket of iced water over them. They got away from me as quickly as they could.'

'A few weeks later, Tanya told me, "I can't play with some of the girls in the class because they say you've got a funny job."'

'It seemed that ancient prejudices were still alive. For centuries, society persecuted people with natural psychic gifts. Herbalists and healers were burned at the stake for practising "black magic". People were denied their natural abilities and instead they were forced to hide them. And now, even today, people's fascination with psychic phenomena sits side by side with fear of the unknown.'

'After the response of those mothers, I felt I had a duty never to deny being psychic again. I feel I'm on a mission to normalize the paranormal, to make it acceptable and to encourage people to own their natural and intuitive sixth sense.'

'So yes, over the years, I've got used to being treated differently, but it's part of what I do. I've learned to brush off both people's hatred and their adulation. The main thing is to stay intact, develop my own core – and be myself.'

* * *

Roz

After Mia had gone, I rang my friend and told her what I'd seen. I'd known her since I was eleven years old. She is pragmatic, an atheist; she only believes in what she can touch and see. In some ways, I'd chosen the toughest subject to practise on. Nevertheless, I couldn't help but be disappointed by her response.

She tried to be encouraging to her old friend who was attempting to be a psychic, but she was clearly not bowled over by what I had seen. She liked Mia's 'broad interpretation' which, she said, could probably be applied to everyone, but she could not pinpoint the exact situation or emotion. My first reading in the relationship room had not been a success. If I was honest, it had been a resounding failure.

As I put down the phone, I felt disillusioned. My old school friend represented the part of me that is sceptical. I began to doubt the powers that Mia thought I had. Alongside my feelings of failure, a new question began to take hold: did I want to have psychic abilities?

I was committed to the journey and deeply curious. It was like being in an exciting adventure story. I was intrigued to see what would happen next. But that was scary too – the noise in the empty church, for instance. Mia was very laid back about talking to ghosts, but I still felt freaked out by the idea of talking to dead people.

On top of that, I'm a private person – the thought of going somewhere and being bombarded with information whether I wanted it or not … and strangers approaching me and then being invaded by all sorts of intimate information about their lives.

And people had such expectations of Mia. After the waitress in the pub had shared the reading with her friends at the bar, I remembered the way they had all stared at us. Mia might be able to cope with that special position but I had no wish to stir up such strong emotions. I didn't want to be put on a pedestal.

I began to have serious doubts. All the energy and enthusiasm I had had seemed to disappear. Why was I doing this? Did I really want to be a psychic?

Chapter 18

—⁂—

Breakthrough

Roz

Mia and I took a break for a month. She set me homework to do in her absence.

'Just before you go to sleep each night, go into the zone and see what you can see. Don't worry about it. Just practise being a non-emotional observer.'

But every time I thought about going into the zone I got a tightness in my chest. I knew that I should be practising, but the resistance was overwhelming. I didn't want to do it.

Up until that point, I felt I'd been playing – but suddenly it was more real, more scary. I feared I couldn't do it. I didn't want to try – and fail. I didn't want to be rubbish. Somehow, a whole month went by and I never ventured into the zone.

Mia

Driving to Roz's, I felt optimistic. I was looking forward to hearing how she had got on. I wondered if she'd been developing in other ways since I'd left and if she was filled with the same awe that I had had at the start.

I imagined Roz as an excited schoolgirl, eager to share her new experiences and filled with questions. I was beginning to think that I had a handle on this teaching. I imagined myself providing answers in a way that was both benevolent and inspiring.

Roz
When Mia arrived, I made her a cup of coffee. Inevitably, after the toast and marmalade, the questions came.

Mia
'Well, have you been practising? Have you had any experiences? Are you enjoying it? Have you discovered anything new?'

Roz
I felt really uncomfortable.
  'I've been busy with other things.'

Mia
'You haven't even tried going into the zone before sleep? It only takes a couple of minutes. I don't understand, I thought you wanted to learn.'

Roz
I could feel her disappointment.
  'I knew I should be practising and that it would be good for me, but it was like school homework that I didn't want to do. I always had an excuse why now was not the right time.'

Mia
I was frustrated. I'd had a five-hour drive to Roz's and I was staying in a B&B, rather than my own comfy bed. Why was I doing all this if she wasn't really interested?
  As I sat in silence, drinking my coffee, I remembered that Roz had not been inflicted with the gift as I had been. Roz didn't have

the desperate hunger that I'd had to find answers. She was coming at it from a completely different place – she was choosing to find her powers.

Maybe her resistance wasn't her fault. There hadn't been enough magic to enthral her yet. I'd been teaching her with the idea that she would feel the same as I had in the beginning, but this was clearly wrong.

'Okay, let's talk. Right at this minute, what do you think about it all?'

Roz

I felt small. It hurt to say, 'I don't think I'm ever really going to see anything. I wasn't born with your gift. Deep down, I think, I'm scared of failing.'

Mia

'How can you fail? Who's going to fail you? Every little bit you do counts. There is no failure – only stretching what you've got. It's like saying you're scared to grow your hair long – but each centimetre is longer than it was before. That growth, however small, matters.'

'There is no set goal, only expansion and growth. The important thing is to be on the journey.'

Roz

Mia's words made sense to me, but they didn't seem to help.

Mia

'Shall we go into the zone while I'm here, now? We can do it together.'

Roz

'I love it when you go into the zone and I hear the things you have to say or messages from Eric, but I don't want to go in there myself. I can't really explain it. I just don't want to.'

Mia

I didn't have an answer for that, except, 'I am going to go outside and have a smoke.'

Leaning against the wall at the back of the cottage, I lit a cigarette. The oracle had run out of answers. I needed to gather myself. I felt I was pressurizing Roz into doing something she didn't want to do. I felt like the parent telling the child to clean up their bedroom. The atmosphere between us felt uncomfortable.

'Okay Eric,' I said in my head. 'What the hell do I do now? Is she right? Am I pushing for something that can't be achieved?'

Eric's outline was beside me, leaning against the wall. We were both looking out into Roz's overgrown back garden.

'Roz is not at fault. She is not a mini you.'

'I gathered that. When I first learnt to be psychic I was really scared and I needed answers, I needed to know how to control it. Obviously Roz does not have that need.'

'The aim is not to make a replica of you, but to bring out the best in Roz, the best of her abilities. Seeing random images and auras is not enough to sustain her belief in the sixth sense. For Roz, it's got to be more practical than that. It could mean that Roz isn't meant to be a psychic. It may be that she is meant to be a healer.'

I was shocked – if Roz was meant to be a healer, what on Earth had I been doing these last months? What was I doing here? I had no training as a healer. In fact, everything I knew about healing could be taught in ten minutes. How could I help Roz?

If healing was to be Roz's vocation, she needed someone else. As I stood looking out over the tangle of brambles and long grass,

I had the thought that perhaps my journey with Roz was over. Was this the last day we were going to spend together?

I didn't voice these thoughts to Eric, but the next thing he said was, 'You know the basics of healing. Trust in Roz's ability to do the rest. She's a better healer than you.'

Cheers Eric. Any pride about being a teacher was being well and truly knocked out of me. I felt deflated. Hearing Eric praise someone else's ability was very strange. I realized I'd become comfortable having Eric all to myself and had assumed I was his special person. To be told that my pupil was better than me was quite a shock.

Realization dawned. Eric was telling me that more humility was required. He was also telling me I didn't have to be the teacher, I just had to give Roz the tools. Throwing the cigarette butt to the ground, I walked back to join Roz in the front room. She was in exactly the same position that I had left her.

'I've just had a chat with Eric. Listen, it's possible you may never develop into a psychic but you have another gift.'

Roz

It was one thing not to practise at being a psychic, quite another to be told I wasn't capable of being one. There wasn't any magic in me. I'd wasted Mia's time. If she'd had another pupil, they'd be sitting in the zone right now, seeing wonderful images. And here I was: not only had I failed, but I'd ensured my failure by not even bothering to do my homework. It didn't help that Mia was disappointed too.

'I feel really bad now. Perhaps if I'd worked harder ...'

Mia

'You didn't hear what I said. You've got another gift. Eric says you're a good healer. If he says that, then you've got to be. The weird thing is, it's not even my field.'

Roz

'Actually, a few years ago, I did a course on healing.'

Mia

'You kept that bloody quiet.'

Roz

'I never really used it. I enjoyed learning about healing and practising on people during my course. I had to do case histories and
write up the results. But even though I got a certificate, I never
believed I could do it.'

Mia

Roz had done a proper training course. All I'd done was try it out
on friends and family. Basic healing, as taught by Eric.

'Do you want to be a healer? Eric says you can. What do you
think? He said all I have to do is give you the tools. That means
showing you the method Eric showed me, but it's so simple it is
almost embarrassing.'

Roz

'Eric showed you? Why don't you practise healing?'

Mia

'I felt, years ago, that I couldn't spread myself too thinly or I
would become a jack of all trades and master of none. I was
drawn more to the psychic and mediumship side of the work.'

'Also, the way Eric showed me seemed too easy – as if it couldn't
be real. Yet if you look at religious teachings, the greatest healers
did it very simply – without fuss or ceremony.'

I sat there wondering whether I should heal Roz or she should
heal me. Then I remembered Eric saying 'give her the tools', so

although it had been at least fifteen years since I'd last attempted healing, I tried to drag up what I'd been taught.

'Okay Roz, sit in that chair.'

I pointed at a straight-backed wicker chair.

'Now close your eyes and relax.'

I was feeling self-conscious. Roz was the one who'd been on a proper accredited course. I suddenly felt like the pupil talking to the teacher.

'I don't know what you were taught, but this is the way I know.'

I stood behind Roz.

'My feet are shoulder-width apart and, if I was in heels, I would take my shoes off so I could feel grounded. Apart from that, I just need to stand comfortably.'

'The basis of this healing is simplicity. All around us is energy – in the air that we breathe and in every living thing – and that energy is free to tap into. Visualize and believe – these are the keys. I see the energy as a thick mist with light in it.'

'I can visualize the light coming into the top of my head or coming from the ground underneath my feet; either way it fills my entire body. The idea is to stand a moment until the visual image is completed and the healer is full of energy. Then place your hands a few inches above the head of the person you're healing.'

'You don't need to touch a person's body to heal – just their aura. The rule isn't absolute – sometimes you may feel a strong need to touch the body. Just remember to let it come naturally – instinctively.'

As I placed my hands above Roz's head, I visualized the energy pouring out of my hands and enveloping her, charging up her aura. I was surprised by a feeling of energy between my hands and her head.

My awkwardness went. I felt filled with energy and warmth. I felt I could help. In that moment, all the aches and pains I normally felt in my body were gone. It was totally the right thing to be doing. Why didn't I do this more often?

'As you stand with your hands above the person's head, you may feel pulled to another area of the body. Allow your hands to go there and hold them hovering, still not touching the body. Visualize energy pouring from your hands into the spot that you feel needs it. Hold your hands there until the urge is gone. This may happen several times in different places.'

'Eric told me never to draw energy out of the person you are healing. Even if you think something negative needs to come out, just bombard it with positive energy. That way, the healing becomes of benefit to you as well.'

'You'll know when you've finished the healing, because you will want to stop. The energy – the pleasure – will begin to fade. Go back to the top of the head and just hold your hands there until you don't want to anymore. As the healing energies go, you may feel awkward and then you know it is totally finished.'

As I was saying this to Roz, I was amazed to see a silver line of energy going into the top of her head. It was six inches across and conical in shape. I looked up, but I could not see the top. The light went out through the ceiling.

I could see from the lights within the shape that it was energy going into Roz, not being taken out. I'd never seen anything like it. I stepped back. Roz still had her eyes closed.

'There's a shaft of light going into your head. How are you feeling Roz?'

Roz

'Lovely. Totally relaxed. I don't want to open my eyes. I just want to sit here in the floaty sensation. I feel as if my body is humming.

Actually, I feel more receptive – like I might be able to see something ...'

In that moment, trying to see psychically, no longer felt like work or pressure. I felt playful.

'Tell me to see something.'

Mia

I could see Roz was back in the buzz. It made me very happy.

'Okay, let's do a health scan. When I was outside, Eric suggested a really simple visual technique for you. Just visualize the outline of my body – very basic, two arms, two legs, a head and a bit in the middle. It doesn't have to be exactly like me, you just have to know it represents me. Then sit back and see if you get anything.'

Roz

'I can't get that image. All I'm seeing are the colours green and purple. They're swirling like oil on water.'

Mia

'Purple is my main colour and the green is practical – teaching, growing, the doing colour. So that's okay.'

Roz

I was focusing on the colours, but not for long. Suddenly my cat Wesley started wailing. He shot up the stairs and into the bedroom. Then he ran downstairs again, darting and cowering. I had never seen him behave like that before. Alarmed, I abandoned the wicker chair and the floaty space and went to comfort him.

Poor Wessie was now sitting really close to me. In panic, I closed my eyes and got an outline of his body in my head. Instantly, two black dots flashed on the outline, they were edged with white. I told Mia that I had tried to do a health scan on my cat.

Mia

'The image you got shows it isn't serious. You saw it contained as a dot and surrounded by white, that represents an irritation or minor problem – not a serious health issue.'

Roz

I felt reassured but I still didn't totally trust Mia's instincts or my own. I rang the vet to make an appointment, just to check.

When I put the telephone down, I looked across at Mark's daughter Hannah's cat, sleeping on the sofa. The health scan on Wesley had ignited my interest. I closed my eyes and got Pickle's outline. He was a healthy four-month-old kitten, but instantly I saw a dot of black, high on his left front leg.

'Mia, can you do a health scan on Pickle?'

Mia

I looked over. All I got was a splash of pink on his leg. I told Roz.

'It's minor. He might come in limping in a few days.'

Roz

I felt intrigued.

'We saw the pain in the same place.'

Mia

I nodded. This was more than healing. Roz didn't know it, but she was in the zone. I was excited. I wanted to stretch her more while she was here, but I didn't want her to know what she was doing.

I knew if Roz realized she was working in the zone, she'd return to thinking she couldn't do it and her barriers would come up. Planning a strategy, I deliberately said something light and chatty.

'I'm looking forward to going to America to see my publishers next week. I hope it goes well. Do you think it will?'

Roz

'I think it will – there's no reason for it not to.'

Mia

'I'm not looking forward to the flight over there.'

Roz

'It will probably be a lot better than you think.'

Mia

'I don't know what I'm going to do with myself. I'm going to have to spend a few days there on my own.'

Roz looked at me with a dreamy look in her eye. I thought: she's still in the zone.

Roz

'I think you'll enjoy it. I can see you walking down the street in New York and it's so cold you can see your breath, but the sun is shining and everything is really bright.'

Mia

She had said 'I see' – but she still hadn't realized what she was doing.

'What do you think about the meeting with the publishers?'

I deliberately used the word 'think' to make her feel we were having a conversation – not that she was working in the zone.

Roz

'I can see you being really happy in an office, high up, with two women and a stony-faced man in a suit. One of the women is wearing a blue cardigan with a necklace, the other has straight auburn hair …'

Mia

It was time to come clean.

'You're doing some wonderful work in the zone there, Roz.'

Roz

'I'm not in the zone, I'm just day-dreaming.'

But whatever I was doing, it was fun.

'Ask me something else.'

Mia

'Okay, do a health scan on me.'

Roz

I closed my eyes, got the silhouette and saw instant flashes in the middle of Mia's chest and in the groin area. Hesitantly, I told her.

Mia

'That's so good. I've got indigestion right now and the pain in my groin – I've been getting that a lot recently. The doctor told me that it's coming from my hip.'

'Now, think about my daughter Tanya.'

Roz

I decided to say the first thing that came into my head.

'She's in a really good space at the moment – confident and happy. I see her in a grey coat with a two-tone fur collar.'

Mia

'That's the coat she's wearing at the moment; she bought it a couple of months ago. And she is happy.'

I was excited. As far as Roz knew, I was my usual concerned self about Tanya. I had not mentioned that Tanya was doing really well. For the first time, I had a sense of what other people feel when I give them information. I'd always been the giver; I very rarely got anything psychic for myself.

'Now try with my mum.'

Roz

Had I seen Tanya's coat? It seemed far-fetched, but I was enjoying myself. I thought of Mia's mum and was surprised by my sense that she was in pain. Even though her husband had died a year ago, she was always cheerful. She seemed to cope so well.

It was hard to tell Mia what I was seeing – I was sure I was wrong.

'She has shoulder and stomach pain, and she's feeling washed-out at the moment.'

Mia

For the past year, my mum had had a frozen shoulder. And she had been feeling down because the anniversary of my father's death had just passed.

'You're right Roz, you're absolutely right.'

The stomach pain I was unsure about, and decided to ask my mum when I got home. But nothing Roz had seen was wrong. She had got several absolutes and one maybe. I started laughing.

'So much for you not being a psychic.'

Roz

'If that was being psychic, then it is much more instinctive than I imagined. It is the first flash, before you even think about it. If that was right – as you seem to be saying – then psychic sight is here, now and immediate. It is almost too easy.'

Mia

'It *is* easy. It's like smelling. You don't think about smelling, you just do it. The same with your hearing and your sight. The sixth sense is another sense. It's not a matter of learning, it is a matter of remembering.'

'You activate the sense and it is there. All the lessons and stages we've been through together have been to awaken that sense but, once awoken, it stays open and it's instantly accessible.'

'I'm amazed. The one thing I never thought I'd be able to teach you – or even properly explain – is the instant switch-over into the zone. And you did it. You looked over my shoulder, as if into the distance, as I do. And with the same ease.'

'Of course, you'll have doubts. When you're in the zone, you don't doubt the images you see. It's afterwards, when you come out of the zone, that doubt may creep in. It was the same for me. It's only with practise and confirmation from other people that you will start to trust the images from the zone.'

'The more you do it, the more details you'll get. And an understanding of what you're seeing will come. But there is no question, now, that you can do it. You are psychic – and now the job is to hone your skills.'

Roz
'I thought Eric said I wasn't psychic.'

Mia
'Actually, he didn't say you were not psychic, he said you might not be. Saying that made us go into the healing. He took the pressure off and allowed you to do it – to just see with no expectation of results.'

Roz
'I'd got to the point where results were expected and I think that froze me. Without that pressure to achieve, I was free to play and explore.'

Mia

'Eric says, "Remember, belief is the key and belief opens many doors. But everything must have its opposite and resistance is the opposite of belief. By being so resistant, you could then spring into being open. It was hitting rock bottom that allowed you to find the key to your belief. When you felt you had failed, there was nothing left to prove."'

Roz

I could see what Eric meant. At the lowest point, at the point of giving up, the situation had swung around. I'd experienced that in other situations – hitting a brick wall only to be surprised by a sudden chink of light.

'I think I've also understood the trust-belief thing you keep going on about. Each time I told you what I was seeing – and so believed in it – it allowed the next image to come.'

Mia

'And in my experience, the more you trust, the more accurate it seems you are.'

*   *   *

Roz

The next day, after giving Wesley a full examination, the vet pronounced him fit and well. The only problem he could detect was that Wesley was suffering from the feline equivalent of piles. The only medication he required was a little bran in his diet.

In the car on the way back to the cottage, Mia was crowing.

Mia

'So, you were right then, Roz. Your health scan was accurate.'

Roz

I could have seen a hundred different things when I scanned Wesley. I got it right and yet the denial, the resistance was still there. What would it take for me to totally accept – as Mia did – that I was seeing psychically?

'When you do a health scan on someone you love and you're sure they're okay, I guess you tell them they don't need to go to the doctor?'

Mia

'Hell no. I always tell them to go to the doctor to double-check. It's brilliant to be right nine times out of ten, but there is always the chance I can get it wrong. You must never think you are infallible and play God with people's lives.'

Roz

'Was there any point in us health-scanning Wesley when we had to go to the vet anyway?'

Mia

'Of course there was. You felt better after scanning him, didn't you? And you were less anxious about visiting the vet this morning. Your soul knew it wasn't anything terrible, so it kept things in perspective and stopped you being awake all night fretting.'

'Last but by no means least, it showed your instinctive ability to access the zone and get information you needed, not just random images. Roz, I think you must give yourself a big pat on the back. This has been an amazing development.'

Chapter 19

The Café

Mia

When I turned up at Roz's two weeks later, I was buzzing with excitement. Over our first cup of coffee, I told her.

'You know all that stuff you said about Tanya and my mum the last time I was here? The day after I got home, Tanya proudly walked in with a brand new coat. It was the exact description you gave – grey with a two-tone fur collar.'

Roz

'But you said she already had a coat like that.'

Mia

'She did. But the very next day she came in with a brand new one and the fur on the collar was even thicker – just the way you described it. You couldn't have given a better picture.'

'And my mum, you know I'd said that she was feeling down and that she had a frozen shoulder – but what we didn't know about was her tummy. Two days after I got home, she was unwell with a bad stomach. Again, you saw the future.'

Roz

Mia raised her eyebrow at me and carried on drinking her coffee.

Could it be true? Had I really seen images from the future or had I just had a few lucky guesses? My logical self couldn't reason it away. Tanya *had* bought a grey coat with a thick two-tone collar. Mia's mum *had* had a bad stomach – and I'd seen these things *before* they happened. I tried to dismiss it.

'The things I saw were so minor, so insignificant.'

Mia

'I agree they weren't earth-shattering events, but if you ask me what happened that weekend, I'd say, "Nothing much – Tanya bought a new coat and Mum had a bad tummy." Remember, our lives aren't always full of drama. Tanya's coat and Mum's stomach were the only two pieces of information worth picking up.'

'Then, the following week, I went to New York …'

Roz

Surely, none of that daydream sequence could have turned out to be correct.

'And?'

Mia

I thought back to my five days in freezing New York. Going there to discuss the American publication of my first book was a life event for me. But, throughout, I couldn't help being jolted by the descriptions Roz had given me coming to life in front of my eyes.

She was actually doing it. It really was working. I'd given Roz a pass card – access all areas. I could hardly believe it – my first student had gone and become bloody psychic.

'You were right. From the coldness of my breath in the air and the sun glinting off the sky-scrapers, to the people in the twelfth floor office. Everything, Roz, was right.'

Roz

Everything was right? That was preposterous.

'What about the woman with the blue cardigan and the neck-lace?'

Mia

'That was the woman sitting opposite me in the meeting. She's Head of Publicity. Not only was the cardigan blue, but she had a matching blue top underneath it. The necklace was metal with a hanging pendant.'

Roz

'And the woman with straight auburn hair?'

Mia

'She's the American editor.'

Roz

I was determined to find inaccuracies. I could not possibly have got it all right.

'What about the stony-faced man in the suit? I bet you didn't see him.'

Mia

'I did see a man in a suit looking grim, but he was not in the meeting with us. He was just outside the door of the office we were in.'

Roz

'Are you being truthful or are you just trying to encourage your student?'

Mia

'It is the truth.'

Roz

Mia was being very matter-of-fact – as if it was quite normal for me to see things that had not yet happened. But my mind was in a whirl. The disbelief and denial were there – of course – but layered on top was excitement and panic and fear and a feeling of being utterly thrilled. If I was seeing psychically, then perhaps there really was a bigger picture.

'You're acting as if this is all totally normal.'

Mia

'And you're acting as if your accuracy has come out of nowhere, but we've spent months building up to this – all our work with auras and atmospheres, healings – and believing. I may look matter-of-fact but to tell the truth, I am getting a huge buzz out of this. I feel like I want to run out and teach the world how to be psychic.'

Roz

'What's amazing me is that I appear to be seeing the future. It seems I have begun to see things that have not yet happened.'

Mia

'Why is it more amazing to get tomorrow's information than yesterday's? You don't know either before you look.'

Roz

'If I'm picking up the past, then I could be reading people's memories or picking up on the imprint of things that have happened. I can sort of grasp that. But tomorrow hasn't happened yet. There's nothing there, it's a void. How can I possibly be seeing that?'

Mia

'Time isn't how you perceive it to be. The future is already written. Tomorrow is only our history that we haven't lived yet.'

'Yesterday, today and tomorrow are in the same place. Imagine yourself sitting by a stream. The water in front of you is today, the water down the stream is yesterday, the water coming from upstream is tomorrow. But all that water is in the same stream – as is our etheric record.'

This is the life that was mapped out for us before we came to Earth. When you look into someone's future, you are getting a glimpse of their etheric record.'

Roz

'I'm having to take on board two things here: one, that I might actually have seen the future; two – if that is the case – then that means the future really is predestined.'

Mia

'As I've said, the major events of your life are predestined in order to give you specific emotional experiences, but we regularly come to crossroads where we have to make a choice.'

Roz

Alongside my sense of shock at the thought I might actually be psychic, there was a feeling of excitement and anticipation. Now that Mia was here, I was longing to test myself further. Potentially, I had a new muscle and I wanted to flex it.

'What next?'

Mia

'I think it's time to go and play – and at the same time treat ourselves to lunch.'

Over our café lunch of egg, chips and beans, I said, 'Remember I told you how, when I first became psychic, I used to go into cafés and look at people's auras. I also used to practise reading them psychically. I think you should have a go.'

Roz

I looked around the steamy café, horrified that I was expected to look into people's heads.

'Don't be ridiculous, there's no way I can do that.'

Mia

'Of course you can. If we stopped every time you got nervous we wouldn't have got anywhere. It's a lot easier than you think. It's all in the eyes. Just look at someone's eyes, remember them as you look away and then make yourself believe you know that person.'

'Imagine it's someone you know and all you have to do is remember their character and what's going on in their life. Then empty your mind and see what images come.'

Roz

'How will I know if I'm right or not?'

Mia

'Oh, you of little faith. I'll tell you what, I'll do it with you. Give me a piece of your paper. Right, this is the plan. We'll both look at the same person and write down what we get, but we won't show each other our writings until we're finished. Now remember, it's just for fun. It's not a test. Take the pressure off yourself.'

'Let's start with the woman sitting in the window.'

Roz

I was pretty sure that whatever I saw would be wrong. But I decided to follow Mia's advice and just play. The woman was chatting to a friend and seemed light and happy. I had images of her sitting on a sofa with her husband, two children and a big dog. I saw a fake fire, a coffee table and a packet of cigarettes.

After a few minutes, Mia asked me to tell her what I had written down.

Mia

'I agree that she is married with children but my biggest information pick-up is her depression. You were noticing her interaction with other people – but that is just her persona. Her eyes showed pain. Remember people put on a front, so don't be influenced by it.'

Roz

It was almost a relief to get it wrong. I was on sure ground again. My former visions had been flukes. I'd never get information on a stranger.

Mia

'Whether the information is trustworthy or not, you are exercising a new part of your brain. It is the same part that you will use when you sit opposite a client. Practice is never wasted.'

'It will take time and patience to be able to ignore people's facial expressions. Don't be hard on yourself. It can erode the good work you have done.'

'Let's try the woman at the table in the corner. When people are in company, their expressions and thoughts flit and change from second to second. It's a smoke screen. Imagine she is trying to hide her feelings. The only place of truth is the eyes.'

Roz

The woman was sitting with two friends, chatting. She had bleached blonde hair and was wearing a low-cut black top. It was very hard not to go with the woman's expressions. A warm smile – or lack of it – is difficult to ignore.

I tried to hold onto the image of her eyes and wrote down that she had no children and was dissatisfied with her life. I also saw her as a bit spiteful. I didn't trust her. I read my list to Mia and she smiled.

Mia

'I don't disagree with you about her being spiteful – but that's probably a symptom of her deeper feelings – the sense of failure and isolation which I picked up. I remember when I first started dipping into people – I got really disillusioned with the human race because everyone I looked at seemed hateful, angry, jealous, bitter, judgmental.'

'It took a couple of years for me to realize these were symptomatic traits caused by deeper emotions. There is nearly always a cause behind negative personality traits. I needed to learn to look beneath the first things that hit me – and that is the next lesson for you.'

'Shall we do the waitress? This time do a health scan and put her in the relationship room.'

Roz

I was enjoying myself now. There was no pressure to perform or get it right and it was fun to play like this, imagining that I actually knew things. In my mind's eye, I saw the outline of the waitress's body and got a flash of pain at her wrist. Nowhere else.

In the relationship room, I saw her dancing and there were a couple of men dancing around her at a distance. I had the sense that she had had her heart broken and that, although she was over the worst of it, she was still recuperating. This time I let Mia go first.

Mia

'Basically she's healthy – just an old injury on the wrist. In relationships, she's on her own and she's trying to decide between two men. But neither of them is right. She'll spend a bit of time on her own. She needs to find out who she is again and get her confidence back after her last bad relationship.'

Roz

I put my pad on the table and leaned back in my chair.

'I couldn't have explained it as well as you did, but I knew that she'd had her heart broken and that she was trying to decide between two men. I got the wrist as well. Nothing more, nothing less, just exactly the same information. I can't believe it.'

Mia

I couldn't believe it. I was hoping Roz would get a feeling or a bit of an emotional reading but I never expected such clarity. To be coming out with the same information I was receiving and with the ease and speed I was doing it, was awesome.

'Well done, Roz. I think you are ready to start doing readings.'

Chapter 20

Subterfuge

Mia

The next day, as I beeped the car horn outside Roz's cottage, a plot was forming in my head. I was booked to take the meeting at Bath First Spiritualist Centre that afternoon and Roz had agreed to come along to watch me do a group reading. But as I waited for her to join me in the car, I was secretly devising her new role.

She finally appeared with her huge bag and settled herself into the passenger seat.

Roz

'I'm really looking forward to seeing you work.'

Mia

'I'm looking forward to seeing you work too, Roz.'

Roz

'Yes, but it will be years before I can even consider doing something like this.'

Mia

'I agree it's too early to put you on a stage, but me taking the service this afternoon gives us a unique opportunity for you to do readings on people you don't know.'

Roz

'I'm not joining you on the stage if that's what you think.'

Mia

'I'll handle the stage bit, but I spoke to the woman who is running the service this morning. I asked her if she would get a couple of people together who would like a reading afterwards. I told her that you would be with me as my student.'

Roz

'They won't want readings with me, they'll all want to see you.'

Mia

'Yes, but I've thought this through and this is my plan. Apparently, there's a small back room we can use. So we'll get them in one at a time and I'll keep them talking for five minutes before doing a reading and this will hopefully give you a chance to get flashes and write them down.'

'Then I'll do my reading and, just like in the café, see if I pick up the stuff that you've written down. They don't need to know what you're doing, they'll think you're just taking notes on what I'm saying. So there's no pressure. Just see it as another bit of fun.'

Roz

I liked Mia's idea. I'd get to see her working with a group as well as with individuals – and it was a safe way to test myself. As long as I wasn't putting myself on the line and publicly getting it wrong, there was no problem – only the delicious opportunity to play with a bit of magic. Where was the harm in that?

Mia

Arriving in Bath, Roz and I got a take-away coffee en route to the spiritualist centre. We were greeted at the door with the information that it was the biggest turn-out the church had had for years. The little hall was packed.

I always get slightly nervous before doing a group reading. What if I can't get into the zone? There are no guarantees and despite all my years of experience 'what if?' still flickers across my mind. Nevertheless, I pushed my doubts to one side and, standing in the street outside with Roz, enjoyed my caffeine and nicotine fix.

Roz

After a few minutes, Yvonne, President of the spiritualist centre, came out to join us.

'I've got two people who would love to have mini readings with you afterwards.'

Mia

'Good, thanks for sorting that out.'

I smiled at Roz and she smiled back. I wondered if she'd still be smiling at me in two hours time.

I took my place on one of the two throne-like chairs at the front of the hall and smiled at the rows of expectant faces. I looked over at Roz, sitting with her pen and notebook poised as if at a news briefing. As we started singing *Hark the Herald Angels Sing*, I pulled myself together. I'd think about Roz later, time to deal with the job in hand.

I was asked to give the opening prayer. I hate that. It feels forced and always makes me uncomfortable. I decided to say what I felt.

'I'm not good at traditional prayers but the reason for saying them is to reinforce that we are working under the influence of God – and God simply means good. Once you believe that there is life after death, you must also take on board that everything has its opposite, including goodness. It is a cop-out to say that you work in the middle. There is no safe, grey path. It must be for the greater good. And with that, let's say *The Lord's Prayer*.'

Roz

After the prayer, Mia told stories about her earliest conversations with Eric. I noticed how relaxed and comfortable she looked. The people around us were excited and expectant. There was a huge pressure on her to perform and yet she was standing up there, sharing anecdotes.

Suddenly the tempo changed.

Mia

'Let's do some readings, shall we? If I come to you, I'll ask you if it's okay. If you're at all uncomfortable, just say no and I'll move on to somebody else.'

Roz

Over the next 50 minutes, Mia gave readings to 12 different people. She was warm and caring and, even though not all the information she gave was positive, she somehow left everyone on an upbeat note.

And her information was specific. She told one woman not to give money to a young man and another to go back to college. She told a very frail-looking woman that her blood test count was changing and she needed to drink more water. As the woman started to cry, Mia did not falter for a moment.

Mia

'Stress and depression make you physically unwell.'

Roz

As Mia went effortlessly from person to person, I couldn't help but compare her to the last woman I had seen doing readings here. That clairvoyant had looked as if she was fighting for information. Mia, on the other hand, looked at ease. It was as if the information was flowing towards her and all she had to do was catch it.

Mia told a man she could see him driving a car, his jaws clenched. He vehemently denied the possibility, saying that he'd given up driving because it caused him too much anxiety, but Mia was undeterred.

Mia

'It will happen.'

Roz

I wondered how she held onto her confidence in the face of a denial, but I did not have long to ponder my thoughts because she was moving on. She told a woman that she was soon to have a scan on her stomach but that the anxiety beforehand would be worse than the actual result.

Mia looked across at Stan, who was leading the service.

'You have time for one more,' he said.

Mia told two close friends that they had a telepathic connection that they could work on. They also wanted to develop their sixth sense and Mia told them that it was already happening and, if they got at all scared, to ask their guides to slow it down.

Mia

'Your guides will only let you go so far. If you get startled, they'll stop and then start again. Trust and believe in your guides. They will always keep you safe.'

It was time for the closing prayer.

'Dear God, let us learn to leave alone the things we cannot change, to change the things that we can and the wisdom to know the difference. May we learn through the troubles we go through and become wise, not bitter. Let us be open enough for others to enrich our lives. May we search for truth and understanding in the lives we lead. Stay safe and enjoy each other's company. Amen.'

Roz

Ten minutes later, equipped with cups of tea and custard creams on a saucer, we were in the back room awaiting Mia's first reading.

'Are you alright? You must be exhausted after doing that.'

Mia

'Actually, I always feel quite calm afterwards. Now remember, I'm going to keep the person talking for a few minutes and not start the reading straight away. I want you to see what you can get. Look at the eyes, not the facial expressions. Remember to go with the first flash of information, don't try to analyze, it just is.'

Roz

Mia's first reading was a woman in her late fifties. As she said hello, I looked at her eyes. They were dark brown. My first impression was that she was tough, at least on the outside.

As she sat opposite Mia, I closed my eyes and got an outline of her body in my head. Two points flashed immediately. Her left knee and her right foot. I then had the sense of an emptiness in her stomach. I thought that she had had an operation and that it was probably a hysterectomy or an ovarian cyst.

As I jotted these notes in my book, I wondered where the information was coming from. How could I be so specific? I must have been imagining it, but no harm done, she would never know.

I then put the woman in the relationship room. There was

someone in there with her but they were a long way away. It was clearly a companionable rather than a passionate relationship. I thought the other person was quieter than her, more mellow.

I wrote these notes too and then sat in silence. Watching the woman, I had the sense that she had had a hard childhood and that had made her strong and self-sufficient. I also saw a problem at her left hip.

Mia

Roz was scribbling away, so she was obviously getting something. I waited until she had finished writing before beginning the reading. As I spoke, I was aware that I was more interested in what Roz had written down than in what I was saying.

I kept my reading brief, focusing mainly on the woman's aura colours and her personality. I deliberately avoided her health and relationships as I knew these were the areas Roz would go into.

I finished speaking and looked over at Roz, who smiled back at me.

'What do you think, Roz?'

A look of horror came over her face and she started shuffling the papers on her lap.

Roz

'I'm just taking notes.'

Mia

Roz was glaring at me so I turned to our subject.

'Roz is my student and I believe she's picked up some information. Would you mind her telling you about it?'

Roz

'Not at all,' the woman said. 'That would be fine.'

She smiled at me. One option was to run out of the room.

Another option was to say I had seen nothing, but with the mood Mia was in, I couldn't guarantee she wouldn't grab hold of my pad and read it out anyway.

'I'm not a proper psychic. I'm only training and what I've written down is probably wrong. I was only practising, not doing it properly or seriously.'

Mia

'Roz, it doesn't matter if it's wrong. Just spit it out.'

Roz

I looked at the woman. Each word was an effort.

'I saw a blob of colour on your left knee and on your right foot, so there may be problems there, nothing big.'

The woman immediately responded: 'That's right dear, I've got arthritis there.'

'Have you?'

Mia

I tried to keep my tone neutral.

'Anything else, Roz?'

Roz

'A problem with your left hip?'

The woman nodded enthusiastically.

'I've got a dodgy hip.'

It felt like an intimate thing to ask, but I wanted to know the answer, so I gathered my courage in both hands and asked:

'Have you had a hysterectomy?'

The woman looked startled and didn't answer straight away.

'Yes, I have had a partial hysterectomy.'

Oh my God!

I told the woman what I thought I had picked up about her

childhood and she said: 'Both my parents worked long hours and I had no brothers and sisters, so I spent most of my childhood on my own. It did make me self-sufficient, yes, and strong.'

The woman seemed to be looking at me with renewed interest, as if I really could do this. She was waiting for more, so I hesitantly told her about the man I'd seen in the relationship room.

'At the moment I live on my own,' she said.

My wave had broken, but then Mia addressed the woman.

Mia

'The man Roz saw does exist – I can see him too – but he's in the future. You'll meet him in about eighteen months time. And, as Roz said, he will be gentle and kind, easy for you to get along with, which you need.'

Roz

The woman looked pleased and thanked us both as she left. Alone in the room with Mia, I looked at her for the first time.

'I thought I was only taking notes, what was that about?'

Mia

'Would you have agreed to do it if I'd have told you my plan?'

Roz

'You know I wouldn't.'

Mia

'But now you have done your first reading on someone you don't know. I think it went quite well, don't you?'

Roz

'I can't believe I got it right – the hysterectomy, the man in the future, the dodgy hip, the arthritis. I'm amazed. Even her childhood.

The thing I'm most stunned by, though, is the hysterectomy – I felt it as an emptiness in my stomach.'

Mia

'When the sixth sense takes over, it gives you information in ways you can understand. If you'd just seen a light on her tummy you wouldn't have got clarity of information. You instinctively made sense of the information you got.'

'Ready to have another go?'

Roz

'Yes, unbelievably, I am. I want to do it again. It feels great.'

Our second woman was also in her late fifties, but she was dressed in much younger clothes and seemed more open. She came in with a friend and they both chatted happily with Mia while I tried to read her health and relationships.

I saw minor problems with her ear and throat, as well as pain at the sides of her body – a feeling that her ribs were being squashed. In the relationship room I saw someone with whom there was a feeling of hesitancy and to-ing and fro-ing.

I had the sense that she was a person who carried her feelings close to her chest. She didn't lean on people but there was a lot of pain.

Mia

I did my reading briefly, then turned again to Roz.

'What did you pick up, Roz?'

Roz

The woman agreed with all my health scanning but when I told her about the pain in her ribs, she said, 'No, I haven't got that.'

There was no time for me to feel crest-fallen because, straight away, her friend said, 'I have pain in my ribs. I had it all last night.

Could you be picking up my pain?'

I looked at Mia.

'Is that possible?'

Mia

'Yes, and that's probably what's happening. These two women are very close, there are no barriers between them. I should have warned you. When two people come in together, it's easy to get the readings mixed.'

Roz

Both women were smiling at me now. It was a strange, heady sensation. I could feel them both sitting there, waiting for the next jewel to drop from my lips.

I told the woman what I'd seen in the relationship room. Luckily, I didn't give the other person in the room an identity or gender, merely saying, 'The most important relationship in your life involves somebody with whom there is a lot of hesitancy.'

The woman beamed at me and then told me about her daughter. As she spoke I felt amazed and strangely uplifted. I was involved in magic. (I also made a mental note not to automatically assume that the most important relationship in a person's life is with a lover.)

Readings over, Mia and I left the church and headed for her car.

Mia

'How are you feeling?'

Roz

'I'm buzzing.'

Mia

'So I'm forgiven, am I? I never imagined teaching would involve subterfuge but, actually, being sneaky seems to have worked out quite well.'

Chapter 21

You Can't Make Miracles

Roz

For five years I had been co-running a monthly writing group with residents at the local Leonard Cheshire Home, Greenhill House. A week after Mia's subterfuge, Jayne, who worked at Greenhill House, told me that, Mike Jake, a member of the writing group had had a bad fall.

'He's in a wheelchair now,' she told me 'and in a lot of pain.'

I sent him a card. He typed me back a two-page letter. In the days between talking to Jayne and receiving my card, he had had another fall.

Mike had had a hang-gliding crash in the late seventies but, despite all the losses and traumas that ensued, he had kept alive a fiery spirit and a fiercely intelligent and imaginative mind. He had a keen interest in astronomy and was a member of countless clubs and societies. When I saw him, I was shocked. He was slumped, his body crooked with pain. As Jayne had said, the light in him had gone out.

As I left, Jayne said, 'I've never seen bruises like the ones Mike has on his leg. What he needs is someone to do a healing.'

She had no idea about the course I had done or my subsequent teachings with Mia.

'I could give it a try,' I said, without even thinking about it.

Mike was in tremendous pain. If nothing else, a healing would do him no harm.

That night, Jayne ran the idea past Mike and telephoned me.

'Mike would really like you to do that healing. Can you come tomorrow?'

He was in his room, surrounded by letters and books and papers. His desk was a riot of correspondence but Mike was staring vacantly into space, clearly disorientated. He told me he had a lot of pain in his left knee and the back of his neck.

'I'll do what I can. If you fall asleep, I'll show myself out, so you can enjoy the peace.'

We talked some more and then I took my shoes off, grounded myself the way Mia had shown me and put my hands around his head. The sensation of heat being generated between my hands amazed me. I felt powerful and clear. I sent the best energy I could into his body.

'The pain's not getting any better,' he said from time to time.

I felt my confidence falter. I was doing the best I could. I so wanted to heal him – to help him. I kept going.

'When will the pain be gone completely?'

The question had changed. He had his eyes shut and his voice was dreamy.

'I don't know,' I said.

By the end of the healing, Mike was sleeping peacefully. If nothing else, I knew, that was a result. Before the accidents, he had had sleepless nights but now the pain also prevented him sleeping during the day.

I sat with him for a while, sending him the best thoughts and energy I could. If wishes held power then this had to do him some good. Eventually, I gathered my shoes and bag and crept out of the room.

Outside, the sun was shining. The countryside looked beautiful, so green and clear. I was on the way to have lunch with a friend and I felt good – strong, uplifted. The healing, it seemed, had worked on me too.

When Jayne telephoned two days later, it was with bad news. Mike's disorientation had worsened. He had been rushed into hospital.

Mia

I was so looking forward to seeing Roz. When I first became psychic, I was switched on without any prior warning or agreement on my part. It was terrifying. I was hanging on to my sanity by my fingernails, until I accepted Eric and he helped me to understand what was going on. With Roz, it was lovely to see someone developing in a *controlled* way and enjoying the wonderment of it.

I remembered how I felt when I was at her stage – as if I had been touched by magic and all I wanted to do was go out and practice. Roz, my first student, was showing signs of becoming a competent working psychic. The difficulties were behind us now.

'I'm looking forward to seeing Roz, Eric. For once, I don't feel under any pressure.'

I was aware of his presence in the front seat, next to me.

'That's good then, is it?' There was an intonation in Eric's voice that I didn't take time to dwell on.

'Of course it's good. Every step of the way, it's been hard but I actually think I can teach now. And, as you know, I certainly didn't believe that when we started out.'

'I'm pleased you're looking forward to it,' Eric said.

He was always so dry and non-committal. Sometimes I just wished he would lighten up.

As I pulled up outside Roz's cottage, I forgot all about Eric. I was pleased to see she had put the big cushions out on the front grass. Wesley had taken possession of one of them and was curled into a tight ball. I lay out in the sun, ready to hear Roz's adventures.

'How did you get on while I was away?'

Roz

I took a deep breath.

'I gave a healing.'

Mia

'Good, great. How did it go?'

Roz

'Two days later, the man I "healed" was rushed into hospital.'

I gave Mia the details.

'Some healer, I am, eh?'

Mia

'Yes, actually, Roz you are. It was on the cards that he was going back into hospital. He was more injured than people realized. But for the time you were with him, you made him feel a lot better.'

'Be practical. He was in a lot of pain. And two days later was in hospital because of it. But you managed to break that flow of pain for a while, you gave him some peace. You wouldn't want to be masking symptoms totally, would you, if he needed to get to hospital? I think you did a brilliant healing.'

Roz

'That's one way of looking at it.'

Mia

'You don't seriously think you made him worse, do you Roz?'

Roz

'If nothing else, I raised his expectations and let him down.'

Mia

'You didn't let him down, you let him sleep. Healing can only help – at its worst it is ineffective. Would you only give healing to a terminally ill person if you could cure them totally? Is there no benefit in easing pain? Is it all or nothing?'

Roz

'All I know is that I sent him the best possible healing energy that I could. I put my all into it – and it was useless.'

Mia

'How can you say that when you took away his pain and he fell asleep? Most people start healing on a toothache or a headache. You jump straight into the deep end with somebody who's been ill for an awfully long time. Even so, you still managed to help him.'

'If you knew beforehand that you could only take the pain away for a while, enough to let him sleep, would you not have bothered?'

Roz

'Of course, I would still have done whatever I could. But are you saying that, because he was so ill, I was never going to manage to heal him? Are you saying there are no miracles?'

Mia

'Miracles do happen but they are rare – you can't expect them every time you lay your hands on someone. Alleviating pain is a miracle in itself.'

'If I took what you are saying into the psychic reading situation, then I would never do a reading for a bereaved person unless the spirit of their departed was definitely going to come in. Do you see how foolish that would be? The most important thing is to try to benefit – even if only one word you said made a person feel better, it is not wasted.'

Roz

'What about the power of positive intent and wishes? I really wished him better, with all of me.'

Mia

'And I'm sure your energy wrapped him up and helped him sleep.'

Roz

'Do wishes make a difference?'

Mia

'Wishes matter, but belief is stronger. A wish has an element of doubt, but belief has no room for doubt – that's why it is more powerful. As your teacher, I'm pleased with the healing you did. You made an ill man feel better for a while, and you left him sleeping.'

More importantly, Roz was naturally and instinctively working from a position of love. Somehow, I had to help her take that on board.

'The most important part of any reading – or healing – the thing I always make sure I am feeling for the person sitting opposite me is mother love. Mother love is a non-judgemental love, the absolute bottom line. And you do it naturally.'

'When you spoke to the women at the spiritualist church, you emanated warmth. You showed that you cared. You were totally unthreatening. Your aura stretched towards them and enveloped them. I'd never seen that before but it showed that the essence of you is caring.'

'The women were older and tougher than you – and I put you on the spot – but, still, something deep inside of you switched over when you started to tell them your images. Even though you felt worried and timid, your warmth was present. You made the women feel cared for and that they were important.'

'You naturally work from a position of love, but it would do you no harm to acknowledge it. Right at the beginning of any reading or healing, I'd like you to make eye contact with the person and acknowledge to yourself that this person has had many problems in their life and, like everyone else, they deserve to be cared for.'

'If you ever think you can't care for the person in front of you, don't do the reading. It's wrong to do a reading for someone you dislike because you won't care enough to ensure that whatever you say is ultimately beneficial.'

Roz

'The mother love thing that you are describing is instinctive. It seems to go with the territory. There is no way of giving the information and not giving warmth too. When I gave the readings, I wanted to be helpful.'

Mia

'In my experience, the more pure your emotion for the person sitting opposite you, the clearer the information. It's wonderful that you naturally care for people when you're looking into their lives. It makes my job so much easier – and your job, ultimately, so much more beneficial.'

Chapter 22

The Psychic Supper

Roz

Friday morning. I waved goodbye to Mia at the front door.

Mia

'You're doing really well. What you need to do now is find people to give readings to and then practise, practise, practise.'

Roz

The sun was shining. I stayed sitting on the front step after Mia had gone. Ten minutes later the telephone rang.

'Hello, it's Yvonne from Bath First Spiritualist Centre. I am trying to contact Mia Dolan or her student.'

'I'm her student.'

'We're having a Spiritualist Supper at the centre tomorrow night and one of our psychics has dropped out at the last minute. I wonder, would you be able to take her place?'

'I'm sorry, Mia has just left to go back to Sheppey.'

'Not Mia. I'm wondering if *you* would be able to do it.'

'Me?' I was appalled. 'No, no. I'm just starting. I only get odd flashes of information. I wouldn't be able to do it.'

'I've heard you're very good.'

Yvonne had spoken to the women Mia and I had read for. She explained that she taught a weekly psychic development class at the centre and had come to recognize when students were ready to give readings.

'I think you'll be good.'

She explained about the Psychic Supper.

'There will be seven tables, with five people sitting at each. At the head of each table, there is an empty chair. You sit in that chair and you have 20 minutes to give messages to the people at your table. Then you move onto the next table and do the same again.'

'You want me to give messages to five people at every table?'

'Three would be good. When a person has had a reading, they turn over a green card in front of them, so you will know the people who have not yet had readings and it's a good idea to try to do them first.'

'What if I don't get any messages for any of them?'

Yvonne was a no-nonsense woman.

'That would be deathly for the people at your table.'

I sat in horrified silence, then Yvonne rallied round.

'I think you'll be fine but if you get totally stuck, I'll step in and help you.'

'Can I think about it and phone you back?'

I telephoned Mia on her mobile. She was on the motorway.

Mia

As I listened to Roz's mixture of panic and excitement, all I could think was, what a gift. This was exactly what we needed. The important thing was to help Roz believe she could do it.

'There's nothing left for me to teach you, Roz. What you need is experience – that's what I said just before I left and now it's being offered to you on a plate. There's no reason at all why you can't do this.'

Roz

'I'll never manage to give all the people at the table a reading.'

Mia

'Everyone has something blaring – something that is psychically easy to see. Look for it and go with your first flash. You're just giving flashes, you're not going deep. And it's easier to give a lot of people a little, than a few people a lot.

'You *can* do it – you're better than a lot of psychics out there. I would put you in front of my clients.'

Roz

'You would?'

Mia

'I know it feels scary, but you're ready.'

Roz

I put the telephone down and rang Mark. He'd followed my progress with Mia every step of the way. He was grounded and real. And he wouldn't let me make a fool of myself.

'You like a challenge, Roz. If nothing else it will show you how far you've come. I know it's daunting, but it's a test. I think you'll get off to a slow start, then there'll be no stopping you and we'll have to drag you out,' he said. 'That's my prediction.'

I didn't want time to chicken out so I telephoned Yvonne immediately.

'I'll do it.'

'That's good,' she said. 'I'll see you tomorrow night at 7.15.'

I'd wanted practice and here it was, in spadefuls. I was diving off the deep end. I'm naturally quite shy – not the type to strike up conversations with people I don't know, let alone deliver intimate information to 35 expectant strangers. I felt sick.

Mia thinks you can do it, I told myself. Yvonne thinks you can do it. I was pretty sure I would see something – *something* – and I had the visualization techniques of the health scan and the relationship room to help me.

And David, my guide.

Having spent so much time around Mia and Eric, the idea of a guide being on hand to help out seemed natural – right. So far I hadn't needed David, but now that I did, I had a quiet certainty that he would be there. And, as I felt the certainty, I thought perhaps my back felt a little more warm.

The next evening I was surprised to feel more excited than nervous. Mark said, 'You can't fail for trying.' My friend Mercedes called and asked to speak to 'Madame Roz'. She was encouraging, believing in my ability.

Twenty minutes before I was due to leave, Mia telephoned with her final piece of advice.

Mia
'Trust your instincts and remember it's easy.'

Roz
I arrived early and sat in the car park with a thermos flask of tea that Mark had made me. It was good to have some time alone. There was a light rain on the windscreen. I felt oddly good. I was nervous, but calm – I knew I'd receive some information, however little.

Sipping the hot tea, I set my motivation: 'May I say something that is of benefit.' Then I thought of David.

'David, I'm really going to need you tonight. Please be with me and help me.'

Quickly, I could feel the warmth along my left shoulder that I had begun to associate with him. Then I felt a heaviness in my arms that I have never felt before. It was as if my arms were carrying something solid. I had the feeling that David was with me – that he would metaphorically hold my hand for support but that he would let me do the work.

I heard the Abbey bells ring: 7.15.

Upstairs at the spiritualist centre, three psychics were deep in conversation at a large oblong table. They sipped wine and looked professional, unruffled.

I positioned myself at a distance, on a couch and poured more tea from my trusty thermos. The other psychics – a man and two women – were discussing fees and the difference between spiritualist mediums (those who see spirits) and psychics (clearly less esteemed).

I heard one of them say rather grandly, 'I start where the psychics stop.'

A text from Mark. 'Practice all you have learnt to date and you'll be fine. Good vibes.'

A man came and sat on the couch opposite me. I recognized him as Stan, who chaired the spiritualist centre meetings we had attended. His voice was kind and warm.

'We don't go on until 7.45 now,' he told me.

'Have you done this a lot?' I asked.

'I've been doing it for 40 years.' He smiled without a trace of ego. 'The simpler you keep it, the better it is. Simplicity touches the heart.'

'I've never done this before,' I said quietly.

'I think we are always protected,' he said conspiratorially. 'I've always thought that.'

Suddenly the man holding court at the main table called my name.

'I can see spirit behind you,' he said. 'A little girl, she's very mischievous.'

I said thank you, because I did not know what else to say. And then it was time to go downstairs.

We were six psychics in total. We all stood in the hall near the front door, waiting. I stepped outside for a minute. It was a beautiful, still night. Full moon. I called David's name again in my head. And, again, I felt the warmth of his presence. With that, I walked back into the hall and waited with the other psychics.

When Yvonne called us, we walked into the main room and looked around, selecting our first table. At the table nearest the door, three blonde women sat, sipping wine. They looked as if they were in their twenties.

One of the psychics – a man with grey hair and a gentle face – also seemed to like the look of this particular table but Yvonne came up behind us and gave the table to me. I sat down and looked at the place mat in front of me. It read: 'Medium'.

I introduced myself and asked the girls their names. Then I looked behind for Yvonne. She was not there. There were seven tables and only six psychics so she had taken the medium's seat at the next table. She was not going to be behind me, ready to step in, as she had promised. I was on my own.

We sat in silence. I was waiting to be told to start. Eventually, uncomfortably, I realized all the other psychics were talking animatedly. They did not need to be told when to become a medium.

Feeling like a contestant on the TV programme *Faking It*, I looked at the woman sitting directly opposite me. She smiled brightly. I had a flash image of her in a work setting and told her what I was seeing. It made no sense to her. My heart sank.

I saw a paint pot. I tried again.

'Are you doing any painting?'

She nodded her head enthusiastically. 'Yes.'

'Painting in your house?'

'The bathroom.'

I saw a ladder by the paint pot.

'Will you be painting up high?'

'Maybe.'

She was glancing at her friends, they all looked a bit excited – as if I was the real thing. I had no idea how long I had taken. I had three to do. Three in twenty minutes.

I turned to the woman on her left. She was more difficult to read. Very sunny on the outside. I closed my eyes. I saw a little red car, parked on a kerb in a residential area.

'Do you – or does anyone you know – have a little red car?'

She thought for a moment. 'No.'

My heart was in my mouth. I closed my eyes. I could still see it. It and nothing else. Eventually, I asked, 'Are you sure?'

'Yes.'

Then she started to laugh. 'My brother has a small red car,' she said. 'He parks it in the road outside our house.'

Was it true?

I had a flash of a train.

'Do you travel on the train?'

'Several times a week, for my work.'

I was surprised – surprised and a bit thrilled. I saw her sitting in the window seat on a train. Sun fell on her as she had to decide between two things – both of which would make her happy. At the end of the journey, she'd made up her mind. I told her what I saw, and added what I felt.

'It may be in the future.'

They were all smiling at me. I turned to the last woman. There was more emotional pain here. I closed my eyes and health scanned her body. I saw a flash on her shoulder.

'Do you have a pain at the top of your left shoulder?'

'Yes, I do.'

'I have the feeling that you need to improve your posture. If you sit straight, you'll feel better about yourself inside, more confident.'

I felt as if I knew her personality, her character.

I said, 'You don't always feel you have a right to say what you want. Too often you let others go first …'

She was nodding. I told her I thought yoga might be good for her. I did not get the advice psychically – it was because I'd been doing classes and found them helpful. One of the other women said she'd often thought of doing yoga and I relaxed as we got into a conversation about the different types.

The conversation came around to healing. One woman said she'd had healing twice and suddenly I knew what for because I could feel it.

'For anxiety in your chest?'

'Yes. The healer taught me a meditation to ease it, but it was years ago and I've forgotten it. I wish I could remember – it really helped.'

'Was it breath meditation?' I asked.

'Yes.'

I had been taught breath meditation in India. I told them what I knew. The conversation was lively now as we all talked about instinct and energy and relaxation. Somehow I was helping them connect with their spirituality. When the time came to change tables, they did not want me to go.

'Can't you stay at our table?'

Yvonne came over.

'Wrap it up now,' she said in my ear.

'We're in the middle of something,' I said bravely. 'Can I carry on here?'

'That wouldn't be fair on the other tables,' Yvonne said. 'You can always talk some more later.'

Reluctantly, I said goodbye to the three women. I thought I'd had a few psychic flashes – not terribly significant, but accurate. That – and the general chat about spirituality – had made me feel useful. I did not want to be tested anymore.

The next table had five people sitting at it: four women and a man. Two of the women had no green cards in front of them. This meant that they had not yet had a reading. I looked at one of them. She had her arms folded across her chest and looked bored. I would never dare try to read for her.

I looked at the other woman. I closed my eyes and saw her in Wellington boots in mud. I told her what I was seeing. She shook her head.

'No.'

I knew it was wrong. It did not feel right at all. I had started too soon. Nervousness meant I was not giving myself the time I needed to set up the visualizations for the health scan or the relationship room. There was such a charge of expectancy. I couldn't do it.

I looked at the woman's eyes. She looked really sad. She was hurting. I wanted to be of benefit to her. I opened my mouth and the words came out.

'You're having a really hard time at the moment. It feels as if you are only just managing to keep your head above water.'

I kept eye contact with her and I could see that I was right and that she was feeling understood. I hoped that was enough.

'It will get better,' I said because I could see it. 'I see you in a really sunny space. It feels as if it is about six months away.'

I asked because, in that moment, it seemed to matter. 'Are you looking after yourself? I know it's hard for you but are you managing to talk to people?'

'I'm just beginning to.'

'Good. That will help relieve your anxiety.'

I thought this was probably enough for her to hear publicly. And I was feeling tired. I turned to the man next to me, fighting for normal conversation.

'Do you come to these things often?'

'No,' he said. 'I've come along because my wife is a psychic. I don't believe, but I don't "not believe". I'm not sure.'

Then, out of nowhere, he confided, 'What I really need is a healing on my back.'

A healing. I was on my safer footing here. I had a sense of relief.

'I can give you a healing,' I said.

I stood up.

'I never relax,' he said. 'I can't relax. I don't want to close my eyes. My wife has tried to give me healings before and it never works.'

I grounded myself as Mia had shown me, and then I put my hands around his head. The energy felt good and strong. I forgot the other people at the table, I forgot the rest of the room. I concentrated on the healing. When I had finished, I moved away.

He was swaying slightly in his chair, eyes shut, obviously deeply relaxed. When Yvonne came round to tell us that our twenty minutes were up, I touched him gently. He came to, with a start.

'I was gone there,' he said. 'Totally gone.'

I helped him focus on being physically back in the room, and asked him how he was.

'That's never happened to me before,' he said, clearly baffled. 'I was totally gone. It's amazing. I feel so relaxed, so relaxed.'

I had given him the healing he needed. I didn't know if I had healed his back, but I did know that I had helped him to have an experience that was deeply restful and nourishing for him.

As I moved on to the next table, I had the strongest urge to run away. I had enjoyed giving the healing but I was spent. I felt like a performing seal and all I wanted to do was go home. I looked around the new table – at five expectant and totally unknown female faces. I excused myself to go to the toilet.

Outside in the cold cubicle, I wondered what to do. I was on people-overload. It was too much for me – too many people in too rapid a succession. I had nothing else to give. I realized the only thing to do was to be honest, to be myself.

'Doing so many readings in a row, I feel filled up with people,' I admitted as I sat down. 'It would really help me if we could just chat for a bit.'

The women and I introduced ourselves and talked about the evening. Suddenly, looking at the eyes of the woman furthest left from me, I felt a connection with her. I felt I had things that I wanted to say. This wasn't a question, it was a statement.

'You're very interested in this sort of thing, aren't you.'

At first her response was tentative, lukewarm. 'I've come to these evenings a few times.'

'You're very intuitive about people. You suss them out straight away.'

She smiled, recognized. 'I always have.'

I brought to bear all that Mia had taught me, all that I knew and instinctively felt.

'It's only a short hop from intuition to being psychic.'

I had the strong sense that she was being called into the psychic arena. I had a vision of a man next to her, trying to talk to her. But I knew I couldn't say that. It would be too scary.

'Do you have vivid dreams?'

'Yes.'

'It might be worth you keeping a notebook by your bed and writing them down. You might get messages in your dreams.'

'The other night,' she said 'I woke up out of sleep and I thought I heard a man whispering to me, but there was no one there.'

My heart skipped a beat. I had seen it.

'I'm glad you said that,' I said. 'I saw him but I didn't want to say anything in case I frightened you. I think it is your guide. He is trying to talk to you.'

Twenty minutes passed easily then, as the five of us discussed intuition and guides and many of the things that Mia had taught me. Mark was right. When Yvonne came over to say it was time to go back upstairs, I was in full flight. I did, indeed, need to be 'dragged away'.

Upstairs, as the others tucked into our salad supper, I sat apart on the couch again. The man who had been holding court at the table earlier beckoned me over to a place beside him. The hard part of the evening was over. I had done it. I was on a strange high.

Over dinner, talk turned to giving readings from the stage.

'There's a slot you could share at the spiritualist meeting this Thursday,' Yvonne told me enthusiastically. 'You could go on stage with Karen' – she indicated the medium whose husband had asked me for a healing.

'I don't want to go on stage and give readings,' I shuddered.

'It's the next place to go, the next step.' The other psychics around the table were encouraging. 'You can do it. You should do it.'

'I don't think so,' I said.

'Think about it,' Yvonne said. 'You can ring me in the week and let me know.'

After dinner, Yvonne paid the professional psychics and I gathered up my bag and coat.

'Will you sign this?' she asked as I headed for the door.

It was a receipt for payment. Like the other psychics, I received the fee of £15.

Epilogue: Belief

Roz

Summer was drawing to a close, when Mia's car pulled up outside my cottage for the last time. On cushions on the front lawn, I told her about my adventures at the Psychic Supper.

Mia

A grin spread across my face.

'I've got to come clean now, Roz. Psychic Suppers are one of the hardest things a psychic can do. Even I don't do them anymore.'

Roz

'More subterfuge?'

Mia

'It was too good an opportunity to miss. It let us both know that you can work as a psychic. I am very proud of you, Roz. The next step is to take the service at the spiritualist centre – another chance for you to develop your gift has presented itself.'

Roz

'The thought of being on stage trying to give readings terrifies me. I'm glad I did the Psychic Supper – it was a challenge and made me feel I may have some psychic skills. But I've realized that I don't want to be a psychic.'

Mia

'You don't?' I tried to keep my tone neutral.

Roz

'I am not at ease with ghosts and spirits. The truth is my heart is in healing. Thanks to you, I learned to trust more in my instincts, to believe in myself. That meant, when I came to do a healing, I had more confidence in my natural abilities. You helped me to trust what I was feeling.'

Mia

'So you're going to do more healing?'

Roz

'I would like to, but I am realistic now about what I can achieve. When I finished the healing course, I felt that if I couldn't be a tip-top healer then I had nothing to offer. You took the pressure off and made me see that I don't need to provide a miracle cure to be of value.'

Mia

'That's so good. Teaching the gift released your potential. Your high expectations were getting in the way, blocking you from being yourself.'

Roz

'That message really came home to me last week. After the Psychic Supper, I got a call from Jayne at Greenhill House. She told me that Mike – the man I gave a healing to – had discharged himself from hospital and wanted to see me again.'

'When I arrived he was waiting for me in his room. Even though he was in a lot of pain, the old Mike was back, with his quick humour, his unquenchable thirst for knowledge. But his voice was resigned when he explained that his physical condition was not going to go away.'

'Then he said: "You helped me relax and sleep the last time you were here – and if I manage to sleep it makes everything easier to cope with."'

'I offered another healing if ever he wanted one again and, to my surprise, he took me up on my offer. We have arranged one for a few days time.'

Mia

'Like Eric said, you are a natural healer and all I had to do was show you the tools. The most important one is belief – belief in yourself and in the power that is there to help you. This is where we started out, Roz. Me sitting on that hotel bed, telling you belief is a magic word.'

'When we began our journey six months ago, I also told you my hope that, at the end of our time together, when you were faced with people's pain and need, you'd know what to do. You thought you'd never have the skills to be useful but now we both know you have a gift.'

'Like me, you can make pain easier to bear. Do you remember our first lesson, and Robert and Louise who travelled to see me from Australia? They came to see me again, and this time I gave them a clairvoyant reading.'

'I didn't think I would see their daughter because she had only been dead a year but, as I was floating in the zone, out of the corner of my eye, I saw a shimmering shape. Gradually, aura colours filled the outline of a young woman standing behind Robert and Louise. It was their daughter, Anne.'

'Anne showed me a small wooden box and, inside, I saw a teddy bear, shiny pebbles, shells and ribbon. Robert and Louise said it was their daughter's. After she died they'd found the box in her room at home, full of her mementos. It was the clearest sign

I could have given them that death is not the end.'

'Then Anne showed me a case under a bed and said, "You don't have to keep it, throw it away." When I relayed this, Louise told me it was Anne's suitcase that they had brought back from Bali after the bomb. It had stayed in her bedroom, like everything else of Anne's – untouched.'

'Finally, I had a very clear image of a run-down timber beach house by the sea. When I started describing it, Robert said that they'd bought a small place by the sea a couple of years ago, but they had not visited it since Anne died. Then I heard the words: "Go there, spend time there."'

'When a child dies, the parents often feel guilty about living and continuing to experience joy and new adventures without them. Anne was telling her parents, in the clearest way she could, that it was okay to live again. By showing them she was safe, and telling them to throw away her things and pick up the threads of their life, she was allowing them to stop living in the "pause" her death had created.'

Roz
'It's been a privilege to go on this journey with you and to be close to other people's pain. Along the way to becoming psychic, I've learnt a lot about being human.'

'When I started out, I wanted proof that we are more than physical beings. I have seen and touched auras and I have sensed ghostly energy – I have experienced enough to show me that we are capable of being more than we are. You have encouraged me to see that we have an ability to tap into a greater wisdom. The sixth sense actually feels natural, simple. Not learned – somehow, but reawakened.'

'I was amazed at the things I saw, particularly the details I got from strangers' lives – a paint pot and the colour of someone's brother's car. I was not expecting visual accuracy. That felt like a type of magic.'

'But I've realized I'm not a visual person, I go more on feelings – so I *sensed* the "buzziness" of ghosts in The George, and *felt* the emptiness of a hysterectomy in my stomach.'

'I don't want to practise as a medium, but I do want to carry on using some of your tools – particularly spending time in the zone. I like the idea of giving myself a relaxed space to trust my inner voice. And separating myself from my emotions and becoming an impassive observer is really good advice – it gives me perspective on how I'm feeling.'

'But the paranormal still scares me. I think you have amazing courage the way you accept these ghostly manifestations in your life. Your big heart can, somehow, take it.'

'As for my guide, David, what I know is that the more I believe in him – just as you said – the more real he becomes. I can feel him now, warm and a bit heavy on my upper arms and my back. And, always, comforting.'

'I would not have experienced any of this if not for you. Thank you for the magic lens.'

Mia

'It's not one-way, Roz. I've learnt so much about what I've been doing for the last 20 years. It has been an incredible experience to look more closely at the way Eric works. Your questions made me analyse how psychic information is transmitted.'

'I learnt that guides tune their language to the person they are guiding – like the way David typed rather than said hello to you. And now I can see how guides use direct symbols – simple, child-friendly. Remember the long flame David brought into that early visualization? It was tall and thin – just as he was when I saw him.'

'People put clairvoyants on pedestals and think they are special. But we all have this ability to use our sixth sense. The more people there are, who develop their psychic abilities, the better.'

'Teaching you has made my desire to start a psychic school stronger than ever. You are my first student. You have shown me – confirmed for me – that these skills can be taught.'

'You've also made me more realistic about what can be achieved. I won't expect to turn out professional mediums each time. But if I can help one person to trust their intuition, tune into others and be more empathic, then the psychic school will be worth it.'

'Imagine a world where sensitivity and intuition are prized and respected. It is an eternal journey of discovery – how to be kinder to ourselves, to others and the planet. It's hard to learn new ways but if we can connect with the bigger picture, it helps us to be our best selves.'

'When I set out to teach you, Roz, I never imagined how much of a journey it would be. I didn't have a set plan and yet, throughout, I think we were guided.'

'Eric says, "The path you walked with Roz wasn't accidental, even though it felt like you stumbled at times. There is a greater investment in this than you or she will ever know. It's time for an awakening, to redress the balance. People must pause and think, to realize that their actions have consequences and to take responsibility for their lives and all their decisions. And by showing them what you do and how you do it, you give them the belief they need to pursue it themselves."'

Roz
It was time to say goodbye. I felt sad – it was the end of a special time. Would I hang on to the magic without Mia?

Mia

The change in Roz was striking. Six months ago, she'd been a sceptical journalist with a long list of hard-hitting questions. Now she was like a kid sister.

We walked to the car and I paused at the door for one last hug. It was then I noticed the brilliant colours radiating in Roz's aura.

'Hey, Roz, you're purple and gold. The colours of healing and spiritual awareness.'

Inside the car, I wound the window down.

'Now you've found it, don't keep it to yourself. Sharing your gift is the best way I know to help others.'

It was hard catching the last glimpse of Roz, waving goodbye. But as I drove along the winding lanes, excitement stirred. Yet again, Eric had shown me my path without me even realizing it. I could see wonderful new possibilities stretching ahead of me. My dream of helping people discover their psychic gifts seemed within reach. When I started teaching Roz, I had no idea what the destination would be. Now I could see there was no endpoint. It was part of a process – a beginning.

As I turned onto the main road, the word 'patience' was crashing through.

Eric said, 'We are not going to turn into our best selves overnight. It takes lifetimes. Life is a journey and the journey consists of days and nights. Sometimes it is easy to see where you are going and sometimes it's dark and you are unsure of your path. We are here to learn. The lessons can be tough – but morning always comes.'

S P E C I A L   O F F E R

Order these selected Thorsons and Element titles direct from the publisher and receive £1 off each title! Visit www.thorsonselement.com for additional special offers.

Free post and packaging for UK delivery (overseas and Ireland, £2.00 per book).

The Gift
Mia Dolan 0007154518   £6.99 - £1 = £5.99

The Alchemist
Paulo Coelho 0722532938   £6.99 - £1 = £5.99

The Gift of Change
Marianne Williamson 000719904X   £9.99 - £1 = £8.99

The Psychic Adventures of Derek Acorah
Derek Acorah 000718347X   £7.99 - £1 = £6.99

Place your order by post, phone, fax, or email, listed below. Be certain to quote reference code **714V** to take advantage of this special offer.

Mail Order Dept. (REF: **714V**)   Email: customerservices@harpercollins.co.uk
HarperCollins*Publishers*   Phone: 0870 787 1724
Westerhill Road   Fax: 0870 787 1725
Bishopbriggs G64 2QT

Credit cards and cheques are accepted. Do not send cash. Prices shown above were correct at time of press. Prices and availability are subject to change without notice.

Name of cardholder   _____
Address of cardholder   _____
                        _____ Postcode _____

Delivery address (if different)

                        _____
                        _____
                        _____ Postcode _____

BLOCK CAPITALS PLEASE

I've enclosed a cheque for £_____, made payable to HarperCollins*Publishers*, or please charge my Visa/MasterCard/Switch (circle as appropriate)

Card Number: _____
Expires: __/__   Issue No: __/__   Start Date: __/__
Switch cards need an issue number or start date validation.

Signature: _____

thorsons element